A Short Life
Alec

only son of Elizabeth & Stanhope

Forbes

Andrew Gordon

ISBN 978 185022 252 1

Published by Truran, an imprint of Tor Mark,

United Downs Industrial Estate, St Day, Redruth TR16 5HY

Printed in Cornwall by Booth Print, The Praze, Penryn TR10 8AA

Front Cover: *2nd Lieutenant William Stanhope Forbes D.C.L.I. 1916,* Stanhope Forbes

Courtesy of Cornwall's Regimental Museum, Bodmin

Back Cover: *Alec reading 'King Arthur's Wood'* Elizabeth Forbes. Private collection

The Author

Social and military historian Andrew Gordon studied Modern History at University before completing a major study of the relationship between landlord and tenant in 19th century England. He has undertaken research at the National Archives Kew, Tate Britain and the National Maritme Museum, Greenwich.

A freelance researcher, he has published articles in national and regional journals and regularly gives talks to community groups on a range of domestic and military topics.

His interests include collecting rare manuscripts and literature, motor sport and early 20th century European art.

Contents

Introduction

Nearing the end of a long day spent working in the Tate Britain archives, I came across the diaries of the renowned artist Stanhope Forbes. Copious entries recorded his daily life: the progress of his work, social events and the more mundane details of domestic arrangements. On September 5th 1916 the entries came to an abrupt end and the following pages were left starkly blank. Intrigued, I soon read of the death of Stanhope's son, Alec, during the battle of the Somme on September 3rd 1916.

Few biographers are blessed with the quality and quantity of primary sources which now lay before me. Fi Carpenter, Stanhope's great-niece and closest living relative, allowed me access to her extensive family archive and shared a seemingly endless cornucopia of anecdotes. Stanhope, Elizabeth and Alec had been prolific correspondents and had preserved letters they had sent and received. In addition the family had carefully archived a wide range of material, including poignant telegrams and fading photographs portraying the intimacy of a blissful family life.

Millions of men and women lost their lives during the bitter conflict which became known as 'The Great War'. They were all heroes. Most, like Alec, were not mentioned in dispatches and did not receive a Victoria Cross or a Military Medal. Alec's name appears on just one line in the history of his regiment's distinguished war record. So why choose to write about Alec: just another unremarkable casualty amongst the many?

Was he, as Fryn Jesse wrote, 'one of the courtiers in the household of God'? Was his life really, as Stanhope asserted, 'spotless'? He enjoyed a privileged childhood, an expensive education and experienced a way of life denied to the 'Tommies' who fought and died alongside him. At times the spoilt 'rascal' behaved like any child whose every whim had been satisfied by doting parents. And yet the outwardly confident young man faced personal challenges and harboured the same doubts, fears, hopes and dreams of every young man in Edwardian England. Rarely content with the standard of his academic and professional work, in awe of friends he idolised as 'true' heroes, prone to fall for the charms of more worldly, precocious young ladies, Alec was the caring son who watched and prayed as his beloved mother suffered unbearable pain and was to become his father's most trusted friend and confidante.

Alec's story is the story of a generation of young men and women who believed it their duty to serve their country in fighting against a perceived evil. He struggled against poor health and bureaucratic barriers to earn himself a place on the Front line. The words which appear on the memorial at Sancreed would sit comfortably on every white stone which stands today in the regimented cemeteries of Northern France, 'He saw beyond the filth of battle and thought death a fair price to pay to belong in the company of these fellows'.

Andrew Gordon
Newlyn
March 2017

Each gave the other a most powerful stimulus

Elizabeth and Stanhope Forbes,
c.1889
The Artist's Estate

I

Hail Little Stanhope Forbes

The artists Stanhope Forbes and Elizabeth Armstrong married at St. Peter's Church, Newlyn, in the late summer of 1889. A long engagement had followed their first meeting in 1885 at a party held in the home of the artist Edwin Harris. In a letter to his mother Stanhope declared, *She cannot be said to be pretty but is a nice intelligent and ladylike girl.* As their relationship developed 'Lizzie' asserted her independence and proved to be a strong-willed fiancée who would not, for example, be cowed by her suitor's incessant demands for regular and punctual correspondence.

Though they had distinct artistic styles and approaches to the planning and execution of their work, they admired each other's skills and shared an ambition for portraying subjects with the rich warmth of realism and, whenever possible, working 'en plein air'. A good friend, Fryn Tennyson Jesse, concluded, *Each gave the other a most powerful stimulus.*

Following a honeymoon on Dartmoor, the couple returned to Newlyn and made their first home at Cliff Castle Cottage, on the edge of Mount's Bay. Here, in the midst of a growing artists' colony, they continued to develop their reputations, enjoying a marriage which, unusually for the period, was to be a partnership of true 'equals'. In 1891 Stanhope exhibited *The Salvation Army* before the couple left Cornwall for the summer to visit Brittany, a region where they had worked in earlier years. In 1892 Elizabeth completed several significant works, including *The Minuet.*

At the beginning of 1893 they moved to a small farm house, Trewarveneth, high on the hill which rises above Newlyn. It was here later that year, at 5.45 a.m. on Monday 26 May, that William Alexander Stanhope Forbes was born. Stanhope wrote:

> *Little chap, dear little man. He came in to the world in a most capital manner. I went up to see her and she was looking first rate, with the wee chappie lying in her arms, as proud as punch.*

The new arrival caused a great stir in the artists' community. Their response was characteristically good humoured and optimistic. Norman Garstin commented:

Alec standing in front of a Newlyn Copper charger, Elizabeth Forbes, 1896
Penlee House Gallery & Museum

since you've never been on time for anything, I'm sure your baby could not be punctual!

One of the couple's closest friends, Mrs Lionel Birch, recorded:

1893 is the date of 'Alec's' birth – that little faired haired son, whose future fills so large a space in his parents' hopes and aspirations.

It was not long before professional commitments took Stanhope away to Bath. The doting father wrote to his infant son expressing his regret at being parted from *the sweetest man in the world* and hoping their lives *shall run in such lines that these partings shall be are events.* The only thing which made the absence endurable was *the prospect of being reunited.* While he was away the recollection of Alec's little figure paddling about in his bath was the *solace of Pappie's idle hours.* The letter reveals details of the domestic arrangements at Trewarveneth. As well as Mrs Armstrong, Elizabeth was assisted by a nursemaid for her baby, Nurse Grace, and two maids: Mary and Sophie.

The family soon succeeded in establishing a happy balance between work and leisure. Alec became a part of his parent's professional and social lives rather than a distraction. Family photographs show the young boy enjoying a carefree and privileged life in a relaxed home environment. In a studio portrait, he poses in the fashionable clothing worn by so many children of his generation: a 'naval' uniform.

There were frequent family picnics to enjoy, often shared with members of the artistic community such as the Gotch family. One favoured location was the woods at Trevelloe, set above the Lamorna Valley, just three miles from Newlyn. More ambitious excursions further afield were often undertaken. Having endured the not inconsiderable journey to Kynance Cove, a three-year-old Alec was photographed

Alec on the beach at
Kynance Cove, 1896
Private Collection

enjoying playing on the sandy beach. Several family friends became a part of the young boy's life. He went for long walks up Drift Valley with the artist Lionel Birch. *Expeds*, as Alec was later to describe them, were to become one of his great passions in life. The artist and founder of the Newlyn Copper Industry, J.D. McKenzie, made a delightful sketch of Alec lying in the garden.

Not surprisingly, Elizabeth, who had a great talent and interest in portraying children in her work, completed a delightful portrait of the three-year-old Alec shown standing on a table in front of a magnificent copper charger. Later she was able to use him as a model for *Hop O'My Thumb*. Mrs Lionel Birch noted, In Hop O' My Thumb *the little hero is none other than the fair-haired Alec himself, as he was in those childish days.*

There were times when Stanhope and Elizabeth were away from home for lengthy periods of time. In 1898, for example, they toured the Pyrenees. At such times Alec was left in the care of his governess, Mabel Paul. Mabel, who was born in France in 1877, had moved to settle in St Austell with her family. It was perhaps her French heritage which made her particularly suitable for the position. Stanhope's dominant mother, Julliette de Guise, was French and the Forbes household frequently used the language in correspondence and discussion. Mabel was also a devout Christian whose life and moral standards were strongly influenced by her faith. Inevitably Alec enjoyed a very close relationship with his beloved governess and she played a significant role in developing his character, becoming a trusted confidante in later life. She not only prepared him for more formal schooling, but also taught him the skills and etiquette which any young man would need in polite 'society', such as the 'all-important' art of formal dancing.

Alec in fancy dress with Elizabeth and Stanhope in the garden at Trewarveneth 1897
Private collection

Alec with Elizabeth, Julliete de Guise (Bonne Mama) and Stanhope at Trewarveneth
Private collection

Whilst supervising Alec's welfare and early education Mabel encouraged the young lad to experience the companionship of other children with whom he could share his boundless energy and lively imagination. For though his class and privilege placed an implacable barrier between him and most of his peers in the village, it was important that he did not become a precious, lonely and isolated child. In an early letter Alec wrote:

> Mabel and I have supper every night together in the drawing room we invite Mrs Gill and Miss Pussy and their manners are most funny to look at.

> I must say goodbye now for we are going to have another supper party. Our kiddy tea party came off with great éclat yesterday.

Young friends included Tot and William and the lively and enigmatic daughter of the artists Tom and Caroline Gotch, Phylis, who sent him a charming little book which the whole family enjoyed reading. A letter written while his parents were away on one of their frequent visits to London exudes fun and excitement. Having reassured them about his health, *My cold is quite gone.*

He added:

> There is a great flutter in Newlyn. Our king is coming in the bay at 5p.m. tomorrow. Mabel is at present making a huge flag to put on the umbrella tree tomorrow. We had such fun this morning we went to Lamorna and pickt (sic) primroses in the valley to send to Bonne mama. In coming back we said we would stand at the side of the road if we met the king and yell, VIVE LE ROI D'Angleterre. The folly is simply beautiful. The well is deep. it is more than 16ft deep.

Surrounded by all the creative energy and talent of so many artists and a remarkable genetic inheritance, it is not surprising that the young boy was quickly showing an interest and skill in drawing. Some early sketches suggest he was keen and able to emulate the character of the humorous illustrations his father often added to correspondence.

Encouraged and taught by Mabel and his parents, Alec quickly became an avid reader. A young Alec was photographed reading alongside Mabel outside the house. His mother portrayed him engrossed in a book as he walks with one of the family's pet dogs at Trewarveneth and sitting with a large volume open on his lap.

1904 was to prove a significant year for the Forbes family. Elizabeth published, in elephantine form, *King Arthur's Wood*, an illustrated story for children. On the title page she wrote, *To My Little Friend and Comrade, Alec. This book is dedicated with his Mother's love.* The words 'friend' and 'comrade' reflect the close bond which had

whose future fills so large a space in his parents' hopes and aspirations
(Mrs Lionel Birch)

Alec in his sailor suit studio portrait 1897
Courtesy of Alan and Diana Shears

developed between mother and son.

The hero of the tale is Myles, a boy who comes to live in a remote Cornish cottage with his widowed mother and sister. The beauty of the wild woodlands which lie beyond his new home draw him like a magnet and having explored them he encounters a variety of mythical characters. Like most literature for children published at the time, the story is imbued with a heavy strand of stoic morality. Through a series of adventures the young adventurer is shown the virtues of challenging evil and standing up for all that is good.

Inevitably Elizabeth drew on observations of her growing son in creating the character, aspirations and morality of the young hero. Alec, like Myles, displayed a boundless curiosity, energy and love of his native landscape. In a small notebook his mother had discarded he wrote an account of the archaeology of West Cornwall and declared, *I love to go to these heathy moors and find the relics of this a remote people of which so little is known.*

In the same year the family were finally able to move to their new home, Higher Faugan. Designed by Stanhope, it was later described as, *What one would expect the home of a famous artist to be. What catches the eye is the soaring white staircase, itself a work of art.* Details from the building contractor's records reflect the considerable efforts made to incorporate many exquisite features, including bow windows and the grand staircase. The final cost of itemised sections being a considerable £733. Alec was old enough to take a keen interest in the work of the architects and builders as plans were drawn up and construction undertaken. The seeds of a lifelong interest in architecture were sown.

The upheaval of moving to a new home was accompanied by another significant development in the young boy's life. The careless freedom and sheltered life Alec had enjoyed at Trewarveneth with Mabel and his companions was coming to end. Although there were, by 1904, satisfactory secondary schools in West Cornwall, Stanhope, who had attended Dulwich College, acknowledged the importance of giving his son a good public school education.

As preparation for what would have been a major upheaval in his life, Stanhope and Elizabeth made the decision to send Alec way to a relatively local preparatory school to board for the two years preceding his enrolment at public school. This would give him the opportunity to become more independent as well as ensuring he received an adequate grounding in the many subjects he would be studying from the age of thirteen.

Chygwidden School was just 8 miles away from Newlyn at Lelant, near St Ives. It was accommodated in The Elms, an imposing building overlooking the Hayle estuary

Me who thought I understood and professed to teach my little Alec the love of God (Mabel)

Alec reading with Mabel in the garden at Trewarveneth 1898
Private Collection

Alec on a family picnic at Trevelloe Woods with the Gotches and other artists 1902
Courtesy of Alan and Diana Shears

which was later to be the home of the novelist Rosamund Pilcher. 'Going away' to school would not have come as a surprise to the young Alec. He would have known from an early age that it was inevitable. Like many boys of his age Alec had probably read the ubiquitous 'school story' books which glamorised life under the 'spartan' regimes of public schools. The prospect of leaving home offered an opportunity to embark on another of life's great adventures.

Alec's enthusiasm, youthful ambition and delight in new experiences were soon reflected in weekly letters home. He describes long walks to Hayle and St Ives, improvements in his writing and getting to grips with the fresh challenge of participating in a team sport: soccer. His youthful interest in architecture is evident in references to the progress of a new home for one of his teachers. He followed his father's example by illustrating his correspondence with amusing and detailed drawings. There were times though when the proximity of his home and parents made the enforced separation at weekends seem tedious and unnecessary. In one letter he appeals, *Can't I go with you one Sunday instead of staying at Dows?*

The carefree young boy keenly embraced the life of a scholar with characteristic tenacity. Stanhope completed a delightful small portrait of the schoolboy wearing a formal striped blazer and cap. A school report written at the end of the first term suggests the new pupil was reasonably proficient in most subjects, though it seems he may have inherited some of his Mother's shyness and reticence. Commenting on his performance in reading and recitation, his teacher suggests, *He would do both very well, if only he would open mouth and give the words a chance!* It also highlighted weaknesses which were to trouble him as he grew older. Like his mother he struggled with mathematics. He also found spelling difficult. But there was one subject in which excelled, thanks largely to his family heritage. His French teacher noted, *Very good. He has a big advantage over the others in this subject.*

Looking back in later years Alec wondered whether he had been a precocious eleven-year-old. When, in 1915, he encountered the son of a Royal Academician he commented, *Llewelyn R.A. was there with his wife and a tiresome little boy of 11 – I hope all RA sons are not like that – if so at that age I must have been 'un petit horreur'.*

Whilst he may not have been 'un petit horreur', Alec was the only child of doting parents. Though they were determined to avoid indulging his occasional wilfulness, he was well aware that his charm and vivacity ensured he often got his own way. Now these endearing personal attributes would be tested in less familiar surroundings.

I must have been 'un petit horreur' (Alec)

Alec dancing with Mabel outside Trewarveneth 1903
Private Collection

Higher Faugan, where the Forbes family moved in 1904
Private Collection

2

The Bedales Years

By the age of thirteen Alec had developed character traits and interests which were to dominate the course of his short life. He enjoyed long adventurous walks exploring the landscape of his native land and took a keen interest in the natural world, as well as sharing in the family's horticultural endeavours. He had become an avid reader and was fascinated by ancient history, archaeology and the genius of architecture. He loved drawing and was already showing some artistic talent. Ever optimistic, energetic and delightfully innocent, the young boy had acquired his parents' keen sense of humour and confident disposition. There were, however, the usual adolescent insecurities about his academic ability and appearance. He also shared his father's tendency to fall prey to what they both described as the 'dumps', a period of anxiety and self-doubt which often led to days of gloom and despondency.

As well as having observed his mother's successful independent career, he had been given the unusual opportunity of mixing socially with many

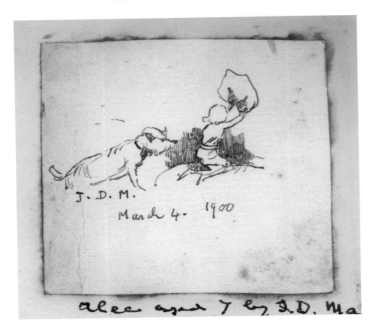

Drawing of Alec
4 March 1900
J.D. MacKenzie
Private Collection

A lively and attractive boy being educated at Bedales (Dame Laura Knight)
Photograph of Alec on the staircase at Higher Faugan circa 1907
Private Collection

talented, liberated young women in the artist's colony and at his parents' School of Painting. Not surprisingly, he was relaxed in the company of women and girls and delighted in their beauty and talent. He was unable to entertain or understand any notion of subjugation or inequality.

His parents had shown him that success depended on dedication and following a disciplined work ethic. The two years spent at Chygwidden had established that he was no great academic or athlete. He was not naturally strong and had an occasionally frail state of health. Nor did he readily display physical aggression and competitiveness. Since it was these qualities which were demanded by most the public-school regimes of the time, it was evident that success and happiness at school would not come easily. The choice of secondary school would require careful consideration if this delightfully innocent, lively, and sensitive young man was to avoid being squashed by a system which glorified heartiness of the rugger field and sometimes forced those with an aesthetic, sensitive temperament to adopt idiosyncratic modes of behaviour which often left them isolated and lonely. While fellow artists were happy to send their sons to traditional public-schools, such as Clifton and Blundell's, Stanhope and Elizabeth chose to send their son to a relatively new school.

Founded in 1893 by J.H.Badley, Bedales held as an ideal the nurturing pupils in the simple life [1]. The school sought to involve the *head, hands and the heart* in encouraging a child's healthy development. This was a highly innovative approach when compared with the prevailing attitudes which still dominated public school education at the end of the nineteenth century. During its early days the school operated a spartan regime. The boys had a large tub under their beds and began the day by filling it with cold water and jumping into it. The curriculum included long cross country runs and work on the land which combined idealism and practicality. Badley believed nature was the best of teachers. The symbolic space of the public school was turned inside out. The buildings had no mock fortifications, nor did they enclose the playing fields. Instead they opened out on the woods and meadows where the students would learn to cultivate the land. In 1898 Badley took on the other kind of chauvinism when four girls, dubbed 'beastly shes', entered the school. As one pupil noted, *Sooner or later you're bound to know what women are like. I myself have bathed with naked girls.*

The emphasis on country pursuits also gave Bedales a reputation among the continental landed aristocracy and their recruitment enabled the school to temper the imperialist attitudes of the established public schools. Steadily the bohemian fringe of the upper middle class was sending their sons and daughters to be educated in this enlightened environment.

Stanhope and Elizabeth's lifestyle and attitudes were far from bohemian. They did, however, have a long-standing love and appreciation of European culture and would have appreciated the value of seeing their son living with students from diverse cultural backgrounds. Bedales was an inspired choice which suited their son's sensitive disposition and would nurture his love of outdoor life, art and culture.

And so in 1906 Alec left Higher Faugan with his required clothes:

2 grey suits for boy of 12 year (1 Harris tweed 1 Homespun)

2 navy serge knickers

3 football jerseys 2 white 1 blue

6 flannel shirts

2 pyjama sleeping suits

12 handkerchiefs (the reason for the large number may be explained later)

2 'Charterhouse' sweaters

Alec seems to have fallen in to the Bedales' ethos with ease and relished fresh challenges. He was soon able to draw comparisons with his preparatory school:

> I prefer Bedales to Chygwidden. Latin is nicer. We have begun Latin poetry Ovid etc We are doing the Merchant of Venice and Westward Ho! We are doing the history of America. I am quite sure I have learned 4 times as much this term as I did in a term at Chygwidden.

Pupils were expected to write letters home on Sunday afternoons. Alec's correspondence reveals a determination to succeed, a delight in new experiences and a wry sense of humour. They also reflected the differences and developments in the relationship between the beloved son and his parents. Early correspondence focussed on academic work and developing friendships. He enjoyed history and drawing, but found maths and latin difficult. There was also the on-going struggle with spelling. In one letter he asked, *When is my spelling book (most sadly needed) coming? It cost 8d to get a new one!!* (**my spelling will be BAD if you don't send it quickly**).

Yet, despite a tendency to be self-deprecating and anxious about his progress, outwardly at least he appeared confident and enjoyed adopting a scholarly demeanour, *I am jolly cocky about myself at geography. I go about now with a history or latin grammar.* He relished any element of competition and the chance to win prizes:

> I have finished prize work and the stencil is all rolled up etc. ready to go to Mr Badley. Excuse my saying so, but I think it looks ripping!! I am writing a huge long essay on

Stanley and if it gets the prize I will get 10/- thereby. This is for prize work. We have to do it all in our free time. It's the only thing with prizes at Bedales.

Early signs of some diffidence as a public speaker was steadily overcome. He was soon delighting his parents with lively accounts of class talks and his contributions to debates.

Away from the classroom the lad who loved the outdoor life and adventure discovered endless opportunities to satisfy his enthusiasm. Long walks with new friends found him cycling to view churches and enjoying picnics with some of the 'beastly shes'. He loved haymaking and was soon boasting of his achievements as an *accomplished* gardener. He delighted in all the new crazes, such as ice skating and playing diabolo.

Bedales offered pupils diverse opportunities to stimulate their interest in the wider world. Saturday evening lectures covered such topics as astronomy, the Russo Japanese War, pictures, travel, crabs and ornithology. Alec's letters, which often included amusing illustrations, succeeded in describing the mood of the audience, the amusing idiosyncrasies of the lecturers and the impact each new topic had on him. Though he admitted to occasional boredom, he was on the whole excited and endlessly curious. He was soon anxiously anticipating membership of the Junior Science Society. At least one lecturer received his undivided attention:

> *We had a perfectly heavenly lecture on designing last Sunday by Mr Alfred Powell. He is head of Kensington Polytechnic. I hadn't a chance to speak to him but Miss Martin did and he said I must work hard at all kinds of designing for the next few years. He had a huge lot of specimens pinned up around the walls. Some old manuscripts and illuminations and perfectly glorious embroidery.*

But it was the *expeds* which delighted the young student most of all. He became fascinated by a nearby archaeological dig and was soon admitting he had spent a little too much money on photographic images of the various finds. One glorious school outing was to Porchester. Here the pupils were able to see a pageant as well as visiting historic ruins. A long detailed account reflected not only Alec's boundless joy but also his remarkable ability to observe colour and detail. It was his appreciation of the aesthetics which lay beyond all he observed which stands out. Aware of his mother's own skills of observation and awareness of detail and colour, he wrote to her, *Oh I have never seen anything so beautiful – a blaze of colours.*

Letters to *Daddalorums* and *Dearest Daddy* were more formal and tended to focus on the topics which would interest his father. Although he had shown little interest in playing an instrument, Alec enjoyed popular and classical music. Regular concerts were described in great detail, hand-written programmes were sent and there were occasional references to pupils receiving 'a good dose' of music. Sometimes the correspondence was apologetic, particularly when he forgot his father's birthday, but as time passed they became teasingly demanding. He admonished his father, who had always been a prolific correspondent, for failing to write regularly. Stanhope missed Alec's company and longed to be with him. Whilst on a working trip to Settle in 1908, he wrote, *I wish my boy were here to fish with me.*

Letters to *My dear mother* and later to *My dearest Mibbs* were more informal and emotionally honest. He readily expressed his anxieties over academic failings and occasions when he had been in a bad temper. Like any boy he knew he could more easily persuade his mother to give in to requests for money and gifts. He wrote asking for money to fund expeds, asked for books and stencils to be sent and negotiated his contributions towards the cost of a new bike:

> *When is the Washington Irving sketch book coming. You can get a ripping edition for 1/- only. I have only got 6d so I can't get it myself. When is Ellie going to send my shirt stockings and suit of clothes? I want them as soon as possible.*

> *Have you got a stencil knife yet! I shall have wondrous results if I can have one by Xmas.*

> *I suppose you'll let me go. Of course it will cost something like 7/-*

> *Would you please enclose in your next letter a postal order for 4/8 because I have been buying some photos of the Roman Villa. They are rather dear but they are splendid great photos.*

> *Thank you awfully for the money. It's very welcome I am saving it up.*

In return Mibbs seems to have given in easily to his demands, though she was happy to scold him for misdemeanours, *By the way have you swiped our Atlas? Fearful hunt for it this morning – you are a young villain – I am trying to work out my trip.*

Unsurprisingly Alec readily falls to using modern slangs and emotive expressions when describing events to his mother. Expressions and words like *closhing*, *buck up* and *boo hoo* appear regularly.

Bedalians occasionally endured harsh living conditions. In one letter he reported that there had been 8 degrees of frost in one classroom after a window had been left open overnight. The result was frozen ink and sponges on the desks. Several letters to Mibbs included appeals for more supplies of lanoline for cracked lips and chest rubbing. Not surprisingly the occasionally frail boy succumbed to colds and other minor ailments. But Alec was always quick to reassure his parents and even managed to write humorously about brief periods of illness. He often suffered from headaches, which may have stemmed in part from problems with his eyesight, and on one school day a bad headache caused him to be excused drill and allowed to stay in bed. Having recovered, he reported for drill and the sergeant sent him back to his dormitory. Asked why he had decided to report for drill he replied that he had thought he was now fit. The sergeant retorted, *Little boys shouldn't think.* Somewhat crestfallen he wrote, *squashed (or despised) and rejected of men I returned to the dormitory. But just now Miss Thorpe came and told me I could get up. Voila!*

There are few mentions of conventional sport in his letters and those physical activities he describes tend to be solitary, such as swimming and cycling. He does however describe with great delight the introduction of 'Swedish drill' session, *In the morning instead of run a lot of us who aren't much good at sitting up and are apt to slouch do Swedish drill and breath exercises etc. like suspending from bar and dumbbell exercises and such like.*

Like most boarders, Alec looked forward to holidays and counted down the days and weeks before he might return to his beloved Newlyn. Two of Elizabeth's paintings of Alec, *Half Term Holiday* and *Alec Reading* show him engrossed in a book. Sitting on a wall in the grounds of the Faugan he is portrayed as a serious young man captivated by the delights of the literary world. Reading was one of Alec's great passions. He loved the novels of Jane Austen, and was intrigued by the intricacies of plot and characterisation:

It's jolly decent, but rather a come-down after my last book I was reading. It's "Jane Eyre". I have never enjoyed a book more, and yet never been so sad and never so excited. It's perfectly glorious. It's not very exaggerated except where she meets her relations (That never would have happened) then I bet she wouldn't have had such a conscience to leave Rochester. OH! Yes, I suppose on second thoughts it is exaggerated and yet it doesn't seem so when reading it.

He also enjoyed modern novels such as the *23 H.P. Daimler* by C.N. Williamson.

Not every day of the holidays was spent in such studious activity. The artists' community was well known for its lively social calendar and Alec enjoyed many opportunities to mix freely with the young ladies who enrolled as students at his parents' School of Painting. (His mother fulfilled an important role in supervising their welfare). He attended fancy dress parties and dances. In her autobiography the renowned artist Dame Laura Knight wrote [2], *At Christmas Mr and Mrs Stanhope Forbes gave a party for their son Alec when I spent most of the evening with Dod Shaw on the balcony.*

The writer Fryn Tennyson Jesse recalled [3]:

> We used sometimes to have fancy-dress dances, known as drenches, in the studios to which the Professor – as we always called Stanhope – and his wife came with their son Alec, a lively and attractive boy being educated at Bedales.

Periods spent at home were sometimes challenging for the usually mild-tempered boy. On one occasion he attended a party at the Bolithos' and met up with one of the Trelawneys' sons. The boy commented that he thought Bedales was a school for girls[4]. In a rare show of aggression Alec began a fight with his adversary, immediately expressing remorse for the trouble he had caused. Interestingly it was his nurse, Mabel, who was most surprised by his show of aggression, *Mabel was quite shocked*.

Back at school the teenage Alec's career ambitions were now clear:

> London University is the chief architect's one. So I see clearly now London will be my fate. I shall specialise in maths and drawing when I am 16. But shan't leave Bedales till I am 18 I hope.

Though he had demonstrated a significant artistic talent and some potential as a draughtsman, to realise his hopes he had to conquer the remaining weaknesses in his maths. He wrote regularly to Elizabeth expressing despondency and anxiety about his progress. It was Elizabeth who took the care and time to advise, and reassured him, urging her *darling boy* to listen to the advice of his teachers and to focus on important areas of study. Elizabeth's anxiety and care extended to Alec's final journey home from Hampshire. Concerned about his exhaustion after a busy term she arranged a sleeper berth to bring him back to Penzance.

In July 1911 Alec passed his Cambridge Schools certificate, first class, having studied mathematics, French, latin, history, surveying, joinery and drawing. Now he was destined for London and the Architectural Association.

3

Getting the Way of Town – The Architectural Student

In 1911 Alec fulfilled a long held ambition and enrolled at The Architects Association. Formally established in 1890, the Association was based in Tufton Street, Westminster. The A.A. had *quite an unusually culturally diverse make up* and encouraged students to *push for an architecture with a social conscience.* He must have felt very much at home

You are a young villain (Elizabeth Forbes)
Alec - in the front in striped blazer and floppy hat - on a picnic,
probably near Lamorna, 1905 Courtesy of Alan and Diana Shears

I wish my boy were here to fish with me (Stanhope)
Alec fishing (circa 1910)
Private Collection

in an institution which had, as one commentator suggested, the *ethos of a bohemian public school.*

Alec was to live in student quarters at Ingram House on the Stockwell Road, SW London. Stanhope went with him to help him settle in his new surroundings and stayed in London for several days. The two of them went shopping for clothes. Alec was to have his first dinner suit, tails, as well as a list of other prerequisites.

Like many a boarding school student past and present Alec rejoiced in a new independence and, at last, a degree of domestic privacy. It seems he was delighted when his father finally left him at last to establish himself in his tiny rooms. In a letter to his mother he described the modest accommodation and listed items from Faugan which might brighten up his surroundings:

> *My bed was most comfy and I was woken at 7.30 by the arrival of a jug of ripping hot water. Breakfast was excellent. The coffee might almost be French – and there were several dishes to choose from.*

> *My room is tiny tiny – but very nice with a little bed, chest of drawers, combined with a dressing table and wash stand and a curtained hanging cupboard – no no pictures. The wallpaper is red with a white dado.*

> *Can I have the photo of you and Daddy that hangs in my room at Faugan? Also the photos of Take these lips ... and June at the farm in my room and the photo of Uncle Kensie if there are any other sketches without a home (or rather wall) you might send one to two along – for I have lots of wall space.*

Elizabeth replied, commenting on her son's struggle with his new clothing:

> *Your letter amused me immensely – especially your account of the dilemma of the dress tie. Do you know I thought about the tie on Sunday evening when I pictured you getting in to your new clothes. And I said to myself I do wonder if Alec has collected his studs and ties and all the things he will want. Well 'experienta docet'. (latin : experience teaches)*

She also mentions how much Meg, the family dog, missed her master, *the weather here has been very dull and heavy since you left. Poor Meg misses you dreadfully. She makes pilgrimages up to your room – and follows me about like a shadow.*

Typically, he threw himself into every experience with great energy and enthusiasm. He was quickly becoming a focussed young man with an exciting new world opening up before him:

I seem to be really grown up much more – perhaps it is only that I am now less of a country cousin – and getting the way of 'town' – fit better into my surroundings and older companions.

Elizabeth's was always delighted to hear of Alec's progress, but never ceased to display her concerns for more practical matters:

as you say 'awfully bucked'! I will look out your largest shirts and send them up by Daddy. There are quite a lot and they look too small for you now.

Shortly after arriving in London he began writing a daily journal. It is a vivid and poignant account of his first few months as a student. In it he describes the progress of his work, lectures, leisure activities, family issues and his fellow-students. In parts of the diary he is brutally honest; he does not avoid tackling sensitive personal dilemmas. Bravely he includes references to his weaknesses and his fears. He includes much self-examination and condemnation. It is the work of a sensitive, and sometimes insecure young man coming to terms with the harsh realities and imperfections of adult life.

In striving to prove himself and to earn respect in his chosen field of study he was anxious not to be diverted by the slack attitude exhibited by some of his fellow-students, who, he concluded, were far too flippant:

I have lived in a land of silly imaginings when not concentrated unconsciously trying to escape realities and moral truths about myself. Also I have let myself go too much – for, it being a physical necessity to enjoy oneself somehow or sometime, I have ragged disgracefully with the rest of the gay crew at the A.A. They are all ripping and I am having a topping time there – but I feel we should work harder.

By the end of the first term his hard work was beginning to bring him the success he so ardently sought:

The end of term and scrabble to get my work done in time – Maule gave me a good report on the whole – but it showed my book work to be much my strongest side. My greatest triumph was being top of the thesis on Greek town planning – Maule really praised me immensely. Then I was second with Funier in the Doric thesis. I did satisfactorily though not brilliantly in the Exams – though a fact which pleased me was that I came out better in the construction than in the history paper. My drawings were spoilt by a hurry to finish them – colour is said to be my weak spot.

Some of Alec's new experiences exposed him to unfamiliar scenes. His comments suggest he was developing a social conscience: a mature and enlightened attitude to a world which lay beyond a life of privilege and aesthetic pleasures:

I feel we should work harder (Alec, 1912)
First Year Studio at the Architectural Association
Courtesy of The Architectural Association

Today we have been down to Canning Town to see Howards timber yard. It was interesting as a visit to the weird part of the World. I do not think I acquired much knowledge – though I did acquire many notes.

It struck me that there was so much more real life and real energy down there than in the vice and luxury sodden west end of London – a huge city pampering to the luxurious desires of its idle inhabitants. In the East End, with these barges on the muddy Lea, the Donald Cruise liners in the distance, factories everywhere, one seemed to come in contact with the bed rock of the empires' strength – and it seemed that even the types met in the street were a stronger set of men than the weak clerks and shopkeepers of the west end.

Elizabeth was delighted to think of her son enjoying the surroundings she herself had experienced in her days as a flapper in London. As a part of his training in drawing he was attending classes at the South Kensington Art Schools:

Mr Forbes has again a most ambitious set of coloured Drawings

San M (unknown), New Year's Day, 1913

Pen and ink drawing by Alec

Penlee House Gallery & Museum

Dearest boy

Your letter came to cheer me up by the evening post – How glad I am to hear the drawing goes well. I should love to see you at work. Some day I think I shall take the train to town and look in on you at the dear old South Kensington It does seem so queer to think of you at work in the very place that used to haunt when I was a flapper!

Despite all the fun of new experiences there were still occasions when Alec experienced bouts of mild depression. He came to describe them as the *dumps*. In his journal he wrote, *Lunched with Bonne Mama – read and wasted time in the afternoon and now awaiting Mabel and Matt – they I know will cheer me up – what a funny thing is 'dumps'* [5].

* * *

Elizabeth's Illness

For some time there had been a dark shadow hanging over the family. During the year preceding Alec's arrival in London, his mother had begun experiencing severe medical problems. Elizabeth had decided to confide in her 'friend and comrade'. Early in 1910 she had written:

I have been seedy. I started with a toothache – which luckily turned in to a little abscess which broke and got rid of itself and then I was no sooner better of that that I got such bad rheumatism in my hip that it has doubled me up. I feel rather too seedy these last few days to make any plans.

By November of that year Mibbs was finding her weakness frustrating and debilitating. During a visit to Vence, where it was hoped the favourable climate might prove beneficial to her condition, she wrote to Alec when he was still at Bedales:

We are being treated to a real Scotch mist. It is cold and vile. I have retreated to a wood fire in my bedroom. It is so thick that I can't see a bit of the landscape – rather a bore, as I wanted to do a little sketch of the old town from my window – Daddy says I am rushing through all the places much too fast and that he hopes I will now let Grasse grow under my feet – but though it is quite a nice place. I intend to move on, on Tuesday – for I don't see what I could do with myself here for long. One can't move a step without climbing steep stairs. And that makes one so tired – so I am going to see what Vence is like if Monday is fine.

By November 1911 Elizabeth's illness had been diagnosed inner cancer and she was being nursed up in London. Alec was on hand to pay regular visits. Watching his mother suffering excruciating pain preyed heavily on his mind. Not only was he now seeking to comfort her but he also felt a responsibility to support his distressed father. The toll on his happiness was heavy. What should have been the beginning of his most exciting years as a maturing young man living it up in bright Edwardian London was becoming a nightmare. The journal became his confidante and he opened his heart to its comforting pages. His words are riven with despair and a longing to come to accept the inevitable:

They came to town on daddy's birthday, Nov 18th and there upon began another painful bout of Mibbs illness – so wearing, has it been – such days of utter despair and pain have we passed through – that I can look forward calmly to the End, if it must come – however I am more ready now – though I write this I know I should suffer just the same if another crisis were to come.

Mibbs weakness has been the 'all' in my mind – I can never forget it. As she is stronger now daddy went down to Cornwall for a few days – it did him a world of good – and he returned to find her stronger.

At the beginning of Alec's first term in 1912 term, following a brief period of remission, Elizabeth's intense suffering continued,

*Jan 22*nd

The bad time has begun again – this time there seems to be no lapse – it almost seems as if the kindest things that God can do is to take Mother away before she suffers any more pain. Everything seems slipping away and the most curious thing about this time is that I cannot pray – I seem to have lost the power of concentrating myself – of bringing myself spiritually into the presence of God – that cloak of darkness seems to have fallen like a fog all round me and I cannot breathe.

After work I go to the nursing home at 7p.m. after Mibbs has been settled for the night and stop until 7.45 or 8.15.

It seemed his mother's illness threatened to destroy Alec's hopes and any hope of happiness was lost in the daily gloom which enveloped his family

Daddy always brighter with her but when away he shows the awful strain and often breaks down. I do too – alone – but generally feel strong to comfort him when I am with him.

Still that awful feeling of void, of vacuum of a world with Mother – I feel I shall be crushed and utterly go under. It is egotistical, but I almost feel as if God will spare her for my sake – for the sake of my work and hopes and ideals. I am in a sort of lethargy now in respect to Mibbs' state. There have been times today and yesterday when I really enjoyed myself – albeit with a worried hollow feeling at the back of my mind – ever-present.

However and awful despondency of the last few days seem to have left me dull and numb. She has been distinctly better the last day or two – though what are these surface changes when the inner cancer is there eating her up slowly and surely.

In despair Alec found two areas of his life which offered a brief escape from reality. The first was the enthusiasm and energy he committed to his work.

*Feb 8*th

Although her illness is all absorbing I must think of my work. I am able to stick at that and her interest in it hugely spurs me on.

There was also the comfort of his faith. For the first time Alec was forced to fall back on what had always been a significant part of his life:

Last Saturday — it came to me as a Revelation from God that Mother is to die. Yet since I have given up struggling I am resigned and have suffered no more. It has always seemed to me extraordinary that people at times of great losses have received comfort in the belief 'The Lord has given, and the <u>lord hath taken away;</u> <u>Blessed is the Name of the Lord'</u> Yet now that typifies my thoughts — my life — my every breath now — I have no longer the weary sadness of those black days in which we struggled with a black and changeful spectre — life is lit up with the luminous Glory — the everlasting Mercy. Now I pray, Night and morn, that as God has given me divine strength … (here two pages have been torn out)

It is comforting also to think of the real true beauty of death — how fair our mourning will be — not the black pamp of shilitons and mutes — but a fair white holy thing of song and love and joy.

In search of some answers he visited a local priest who wrote to him:

Dear Alick (sic)

I was so glad we had a talk the other day — come to me if ever I can be of the <u>slightest</u> use or comfort — I think continually of you all. Prayer is the only thing. <u>If you</u> are ever asked to read the Bible to your mother do. If possible read her St John XIV that chapter is such a help I think,

Yours sincerely, C Turner

Stanhope was aware of the pressure Alec was experiencing. In a letter dated 14th Feb he wrote,

I wonder if you are with her today and I do hope she keeps well. I hope you are looking after yourself as well as after her. It must be bitter in London now. Fortunately cold doesn't seem to affect her. You must be glad of your electric heater.

Even at this stage in her illness Stanhope remained cautiously optimistic, *it will be such a gain if this improvement keeps on and she can sit up. But she mustn't do too much at first.*

Just a month later, after what must have proved a distressing and muddled term at the A.A., Alec joined Mibbs and his father on the overnight train back to their beloved Cornwall.

On March 12 Stanhope wrote of sharing a sleeper berth with Alec, *Everything went admirably on the journey and I do not think my dear one suffered any great inconvenience.*

Elizabeth died at Higher Faugan just four days later.

In a letter to Mabel Gibbs, Elizabeth's nurse, Nurse Kelly, wrote:

> *Mrs Forbes passed away very peacefully on Saturday night. She just smiled happily to us all right to the end. For several days of course she had not been quite clear but fortunately all her delusions were very happy ones. She suffered very little we think.*
>
> *Mr Forbes has kept up splendidly. Of course he breaks down at times, but at present there is so much to see to, that it is a good thing. Alec is fine and has been all along poor chap. It was quite heart-rending to see him taking care of his daddy all along.*

The loss of his mother came as a great blow to the young man. No one understood the relationship between mother and son better than his father: *When his mother died he came through that awful trial I know the gap in his life would be a dreadful one.*

Elizabeth left an estate valued at £5341. In it she made a generous bequest to her son and, in so doing, indicated the significant role he had played in her life:

> *I give to my son William Alexander Stanhope Forbes on his attaining the age of twenty-one years the remainder of my pictures and all my furniture, jewellery and trinkets. And one third of the residue of the estate.*

The conclusion of the long period of anguish and despair must have come as something of a relief for Alec, who had spent long nights observing his mother's pain. Shortly after Elizabeth's death Stanhope wrote, *Alec is wonderfully well … and keeps out of doors a great deal in the garden.*

The loss of Elizabeth led to a steady change in the relationship between father and son. Stanhope had lost the *dear dear wife* who had always been a caring, loving partner as well as providing significant professional support. The success of the School of Painting had owed much to her practical supervision and boundless energy. Anxious to protect his grieving father from unnecessary worries, Alec now adopted the role of a caring friend or brother.

Mibbs had been a loving mother to Alec and he had come to rely on her for guidance in his career and emotional development. Her sense of humour and sound common sense had provided him with a delightful outlook on life's high and lows.

* * *

Alec returned to his studies in London and prepared for examinations at the Architectural Association. Now freed from incessant concerns about Mibbs, he was able to concentrate on his studies and began to enjoy a lifestyle which had for so long been tempered by responsibility and grieving.

Acutely aware of his son's propensity to follow his mother's example in adopting a frenetic work ethic, Stanhope began urging him to take more care over his physical well-being as he returned to his studies, *Do not forget to get your medicine and begin it at once.*

Soon the combination of hard work, anxiety about progress and a hectic social life was exhausting Alec. His father, who had always been aware of his son's frail health and may have had in my mind the heavy toll hard work had had on Elizabeth, advised, *You are evidently working hard and at high pressure and when you have an afternoon off I am sure you should rest and take some quiet out of doors exercise.*

The sophisticated world of the London theatre offered a wonderful escape from the daily grind of his studies, as well as all the delights of pretty young actresses. Following an evening spent watching 'Romance', a *charming play*, he purchased a picture of one of the actresses, Doris Keane, and hung it on his wall. She was not the only actress to attract his attention, *In the evening I saw Sarah Bernhardt as Joan of Arc. She looked a girl, and acted wonderfully – though obviously passé.*

Visits to the theatre exposed the young man to temptations of the flesh which sometimes left him with feelings he struggled, often unsuccessfully, to overcome:

> *In the evening, feeling an overwhelming desire for the theatre, I made for the Lyceum and saw Laraine in* Man and Superman. *What a foray. I had to walk part of the way home – for I was so excited – and I fear it had rather disastrous consequences.*

The gay social life in London brought him into contact with many eligible girls, *I dined with the Taylors – and flirted with a most amusing Miss Alymyham – was she only pulling my leg!!* The family observed Alec's encounters and occasionally expressed their concern:

> *I am so glad for I was afraid that he was going to be caught by that noisy Wilkinson girl. The daughter of the professor of War who writes in* The Times *and the* Daily Mail.

In the absence of Elizabeth's advice and support Alec was fortunate to be able to continue his close relationship with the governess who had played such an important role in moulding the young boy's character. Mabel had married a shipping pilot, Matt Gibbs. She was now living near London and was able to take a keen interest in the

progress of the young man's life in the city:

*Just had the afternoon with Mabel. She is very bucked at Matt's success in his exam.
— the pilotry is now a permanency and so all is really secure now.*

*Saturday was wet. So after lunch Matt went off to bed and we talked hard by the
fire. Matt was on night duty; and Mabel was as usual full of their sorrows. It's hard to
know who is right — Mabel or Uncle Billy — the truth as usual I suppose lies between
the two.*

Mabel was proud of Alec's academic achievements:

*I understand so from Louise also that you had passed your exams — many
congratulations dear Alec — and all good wishes to you also from Matt who says, 'By*

Jove Alec is of the right sort. He shirks nothing – here's good luck to him'.

It was Mabel who guided him through his early romantic experiences, Occasionally Alec became the object of frivolous gossip. Mabel knew him well and was always ready to offer advice:

Louise told me that Duffy Jowett had said that if you and the little Wheeler girl made a match of it he would settle 5000 on your heads at once. But don't you do it unless she is absolutely up to sample. I know jolly well that when you choose a partner for life dear it's not her income that will interest you in the least but don't be in a hurry no matter whom you may meet.

It was not long before he met one lady who succeeded in capturing his undivided attention. The Forbes 'family' home at 167 Maida Vale was not far away from Ingram House and Alec frequently dined there, finding some respite from his academic studies. It was here that he was introduced to his cousin, May. Born in 1878, May was the illegitimate daughter of Lady Mary Rodin and James Staats Forbes, Stanhope's uncle. On his first meeting the 19-year-old Alec, was immediately smitten. It was not long before he was recording his admiration:

May Forbes took me to Bunty – I enjoyed the evening immensely as she is after Mibbs the most splendid woman I know. I have only met her ½ dozen times and yet I am completely at her feet – I am sure she and I are very much in harmony.

He was soon able to affirm that he had formed a 'close' relationship with her:

I am dining tonight however at the hotel with a very charming chaplain called Burrows – a nephew of the Bishop of Truro and a son of the Bishop of Sheffield – he was greatly amazed when I told him I was 'attached' to May Forbes – 'Oh ! yes I know of May Forbes – 'charming and most energetic worker'.

Alec sought to spend as much time as possible with May, though often their attempts to be together were frustrated by other commitments. The *fates*, as he called them, were to blame:

My Dearest May

It is really perfectly sickening that the Fates have been all against another weekend together for us in the Forest.

There were other distractions open to an adventurous young man with means. Motor cars were becoming popular. As a one of the 'modern' young men Alec decided to learn to drive a motor car and wrote amusingly of his experiences:

The motor driving goes very well. – he (the instructor) allowed me into Oxford Street today and I barged about capitally though rather tipsily among the buses and taxis. I am apt to look a little worried and pained on these occasions, and once caught sight of an onlooker very much amused – I wanted badly to charge into him. So far the casualty list consists of one terrier, one old lady and the car itself that was bought round a sharp corner in Gt Portland St. into a huge dray? – but joking aside my most careful teacher prevents anything from going wrong not as I thought – by magic and fine art but by having a spare set of little levers and clutches under his (the passenger's) seat! So while I am in the chauffeur's seat I imagined that I was doing it all myself so nicely, really most of it is being done by this guiding hand under the car – so you see that I am quite safe.

Nothing however was more important to Alec than achieving his career ambitions. As ever the insecure student was anxious to please his tutors and, as he had been at school, he was highly competitive in every aspect of his work. In one letter to his father he was delighted to record:

I got a letter from the Chief, which gave me much pleasure I feel I am becoming in his eyes, more worthy of this great school.

Alec became one of the A.A.'s most promising students. One of his contemporaries asserted that no one who came into touch with him could fail to be impressed by his totally unaffected and inspiriting enthusiasm and joie de vivre. He possessed, it was said, a nature so full of unassuming kindness and 'boyishness' of a character which is rarely met with. [6]

In 1913, his second year at the A.A., Alec entered some of his drawings in a competition:

4 Holly Mount

My Dearest Dad

With the most parlous rush we have finished all our drawings today and now at this very hour the Council are 'sitting' on our drawings. It will be most thrilling to hear tomorrow what happens – We have all today had a great hanging up of all our work – the masters gave us our places and I was quite pleased to have the centre wall to myself. The 'Council Office drawings that I was at in the Easter vac look quite well now – and Cotehele and Godolphin look quite well – But of course I have not secured the studentship. I was very sad at first but now really feel very philosophical about it – for I know I have learnt a great deal at Westminster – yet my work remains somewhat superficial and "painty"–they give me centre walls and little honours because Cotehele and the Council Offices and the splash painted ceilings

You helped him bear the great sorrow of his life. Your friendship has to a great extent made our dear boy what he was (Mabel to May)

May Forbes, Alec's cousin

I am completely at her feet Private collection

and things look bright and flashy— but I know my draughtsmanship remains very weak and design is only just beginning to come — I must do lots of hard and fast pencil and ink work and avoid colour for a bit — we will hear tomorrow about the prizes but I am sure they have gone elsewhere.

The criticism he received reflected a tendency to draw in an artistic manner at the expense of pure draughtsmanship. In this he clearly showed the talent he had inherited from Mibbs and Stanhope,

Mr Stanhope Forbes set is coloured throughout, though he shows no detail, which is a pity. His colour sense is vigorous. Mr Forbes again has a most ambitious set of coloured drawings, which merit much praise. The ideal at which he is aiming is

apparent, but there is no short cut to it. Everything must be worked out, line upon line, and the drawing underneath is the thing that matters. We have no doubt in the future he will realise his ambitions.

In 1914 Alec entered a second competition.

Stanhope recalled:

Towards the end of July 1914 Alec had been working very hard at the Architectural Association in a competition for a scholarship, although his health had been far from good he had most pluckily persevered and had managed to finish his set of drawings. He wrote to me about this time from Holly Mount where he was lodging telling me that the work was done and he had been engaged hanging it on the walls of the A.A. for the inspection of the council. He wrote rather despondently about it. These were the last days of his three-year course at the association and he was desperately keen to come out well and finish with honour he had evidently worked himself into a nervous condition.

The prize was a travel scholarship.

My Dearest Dad

The most wonderful thing has happened. By all that's mysterious I believe I have the travelling studentship — I think it's £50 — I swore that if I got it I should go to Athens and Sicily and all the ancient glories of the World shall be mine. Isn't it quite extraordinarily thrilling — when we got to the AA this morning rumours were abroad and even the office boy knew what the Council had decided but even he wouldn't let on — I have never spent such a nerve racking day of suspense until the little master thinking me going off my head had to drop the broadest hint then he sent me off to walk on the heath and keep cool — I rushed into May's office and she kept me some time to calm me down and then phoned to Aunt Louise who was quite ripping — she was evidently frightfully excited and counselled coolness too.

Stanhope was thrilled:

16 July

Higher Faugan

Dearest Alec

I was immensely delighted with your news last night.

I am waiting now very anxiously to hear with absolute certainty — I do hope however that if anything unforeseen happens you won't be too disappointed. From what you tell me it looks most promising for I can't think the master would have given you a hint, had there been any doubt. But for all that I am longing to hear further and do hope you will write to me the moment the result is announced. I can't quite read your figures and am not sure about the values of the scholarship, not that is of much account. The great thing will be to win it for I am sure it will be a splendid thing for you – Such a capital start and so jolly to think it is the first money you have earned.

Ever yours Stan

Bonne Mama is delighted.

Alec was never able to take up his prize and enjoy travelling through Europe. Nor was he was destined to follow the career he so loved. The conclusion of his final term at the A.A. came just weeks before Europe was thrown into an orgy of destruction.

2nd year Architectural Association certificate.
Penlee House Gallery & Museum

4

Ought I To Go? [7] – Hostilities

By July 1914 rumours of an impending war dominated the country. Events in the Balkans made an outbreak of hostilities appear inevitable. Stanhope wrote:

Each day the position grew more and more serious. News was coming daily of the serious state of affairs in the Balkans, caused by the murder of the Austrian Archduke, and how Austria encouraged by Germany was demanding impossible terms from Servia, how Russia was mobilising and France preparing to stand by her ally.

One Sunday afternoon I well remember, the 2nd August 1914. It was the fateful day when war was imminent, a fine lovely summer day, peaceful and calm.

Stanhope clung to the hope that Alec would never have to serve in the conflict and felt it was his duty to save him from doing anything rash and taking an irrevocable step. Sensitive to his father's feelings and wishing to spare him unnecessary distress, Alec tried to avoid the subject, but his determination was growing as news became bleaker with each passing day. Finally Alec declared his mind was set on going to London to see what unit he could get into.

In despair Stanhope arranged for a medical examination to be carried out by a Doctor Fenwick, who declared Alec unfit for military service. A gland in his neck which had been causing him some trouble had to be removed. Five weeks after the outbreak of war an operation on Alec's neck was performed in London. Stanhope recorded:

He bore it wonderfully well and pluckily. It was performed by the great kindness of his Uncle and Aunt at Maida Vale instead of having to take him to a nursing home.

I remember how when I went in to see him a few hours after it had been done, he looked up from the bed where he lay all bandaged and whispered that he had come from Mons.

Father and son travelled to Yorkshire where Alec could recuperate:

He was by this time beginning to feel strong enough to do some work and he used to draw a good deal but I was afraid of allowing him to tire himself and of an evening we used to retire the two of us to a little back room of the hotel where he could lie down and rest whilst his father read to him. He loved to be read to and we spent many happy hours together. Almost forgetting the war and the uncertain future. We painted the bridge together, he making and excellent water colour drawing of it.

On a visit to York Alec drew a fine picture of one the Minster's windows. Cousin May joined them in Yorkshire and stayed on with Alec when Stanhope returned to Newlyn. The two of them enjoyed long discussions as they walked across the Moors. One of the subjects they explored was their religious beliefs. Since childhood Alec had regularly attended Sancreed Church with his parents. The young boy sat patiently listening to long, sometimes opaque sermons and observed the traditional rites of the Anglican Communion. At home his governess, Mabel, had shared with him her own strongly held convictions, *I who understood and professed to teach my little Alec the love of God.* (letter from Mabel to May September 1916).

By the time Alec left Bedales he had developed a strong Christian faith, praying regularly and finding comfort and encouragement in the study of scripture. His faith was to play a vital role in giving him the strength to face the many anxious days spent observing his mother's illness. When the pain of looking on became almost too much to endure he turned to a local clergyman for advice and support. In his journal he described the agony of being *unable to pray* and experiencing the troubling inability of bringing himself *spiritually in to the presence of God.*

Now the 'evangelical' May and a local Yorkshire clergyman encouraged him to take an opportunity to go on a brief retreat. Stanhope knew that this would not be the first time Alec has gone on a retreat and remained slightly sceptical. He urged caution:

18 Nov 1914

Dearest Alec

Although I won't go so far as to think you quite mad I certainly would consider you a bit dotty. But joking apart I think you know yourself it wasn't very wise to accept the invitation of this Father Figgis to go and spend a weekend in Leeds of all places and in a monastery. I return a very clear recollection of your experiences when you elected to go and spend a similar week end at some sort of retreat and how you told me afterwards you were perished with cold and altogether found the visit most unpleasant. Certainly it seems to me that as your health is the absolute first consideration now you might to have declined. However I will wait till I hear from you again, only please write at once upon returning to Ilkley and tell me how you have fared to reassure me. I am picturing you on a plank bed, in a cell and feel very miserable about you. Perhaps my own feelings have a good deal to do with it for I have been very depressed these last few days

When Alec later decided he wished to be confirmed it was Mabel who urged him to ignore any doubts his father was expressing about the decision:

And now Alec I wanted to answer at once the letter you last wrote me telling me that you were going to be confirmed. I was so glad dear and I have thought much of you lately I wonder if you have been to Truro. I feel sure you will find great comfort and help in the communion service and I am glad to know that you will attend it now – I am glad you are telling the 'family'; they don't understand or they would show no signs of opposition but in these matters it is far better to keep one's own counsel.

Following his confirmation at Ilkley Chapel, Alec was keen to make some tangible contribution to the little church which had played an important role in nurturing his faith:

When I left home after my confirmation I asked Stona if I could give some sort of a gift to the little church. He admitted that they were badly in need of a new Altar frontal – so I tackled May and she set me on to a church concern that deals with such things. Now I hear the Frontal is finished [8]. *I insisted on a white Frontal with sprays of gorse in gold and yellow embroidery round a Lamb and Flag. May saw the Frontal a day or so ago and says that it is a great success. I had some difficulty in persuading the good ladies of the Guild that gorse is more characteristic of a moorland Parish than vine leaves or lilies. But they got underway and I believe it will look very well with the yellow and grey tone of the old church. Don't be alarmed about the pennies. It isn't at all a magnificently or costly affair.*

On his eventual return to Newlyn from Yorkshire Alec attempted to keep himself usefully occupied. Stanhope wrote:

I think his mind was set on other things far removed from his loved profession. But he made a brave effort and used to go down and draw at my school as he thought it a good opportunity to improve his technique in figure drawing.

He also made some admirable water colour drawings in the country side around here. I think it was then he painted Ding Dong mine and several other very clever and promising drawings which I greatly love.

One helpful distraction came in the form of wedding plans. Though he remained loyal to the memory of his beloved mother, Alec recognised that his father needed love, support and care and was delighted to hear of his father's decision to remarry. Maudie Palmer had been a student at the school of art run by Elizabeth and Stanhope. She became a good friend of Elizabeth and her musical abilities endeared her to 'the professor'. She was soon paying regular visits to Faugan to participate in both impromptu and planned musical events. Elizabeth recorded:

> Daddy, Miss Stapley and Maudie are hard at it in the studio practising a trio – and I had an incursion of gushing ladies just at tea time.

The marriage took place on April 8 at St Barnabus Church, Bexhill. Alec gave Maudie jewellery (a necklace) as a wedding gift. Maudie enjoyed her new role in supporting her husband and his energetic son. Alec admired her homemaking skills:

> How topping Faugan was looking. I never told Maudie how ripping I found all the new cushions and curtains and bathroom walls. You too daddalorums looked very well which also testifies to Maudie's good housekeeping.

Stanhope clearly appreciated the care his new wife took to keep him comfortable:

> I am keeping quite well and dear Maudie is so sweet and good and tends me so carefully

He was soon recording how life at Faugan was developing under its new mistress,

> We are expecting some students to tea so must hie me down to don my best apparel. Maudie is glad you approve of the chicken scheme. We have got a cat. Your own Stan

> Here all is well and Maudie and I are settling down.

By the end of April Alec was fully recovered from his operation and his mind turned again to thoughts of playing a role in the war that was raging across the Channel. Stanhope was aware that nothing would now deter his son from seeking to enlist. In his journal he wrote:

> I could not stop my son. I fear I often caused him great sorrow for I could not hide my feelings on the matter.

Stanhope's brother, Sir William Forbes, a director of the London, Brighton and South Coast Railway, found his nephew a 'safe' posting on the staff of the Railway Forwarding Office. Alec's ability to speak fluent French made him an ideal candidate, though the assertion that the young man had received some military training and had experience of Military work (possibly an allusion to his experience as a member of the OTC at Bedales) seems a little spurious. Stanhope commented:

Alec was enchanted at the idea of getting a commission in the army and of being above all able to get out to France at once, and had fully made up his mind to endeavour to do full justice to the opening his uncle's kindness had given him.

While he awaited confirmation from the War Office, Alec stayed at the family house in Maida Vale and filled his days with entertaining diversions.

I continue with great vim to drive a car. The only mishap this morning was holding up the entire traffic in Oxford Circus while I jammed on a wrong pedal with the dire result of stopping the car – Little Overend, the chauffeur was very bored with me and did not get over it until we were back in the garage (22 April 1915).

adding on the 23 April:

I fairly barged about the traffic today and ran a milk cart horse down, of course it was the horse's fault, tho the driver didn't think so.

On the same day Alec was told to report at last to the War Office where his application for a commission was processed amidst a flurry of staff officers and scouts rushing along the corridors:

After reading my papers and talking a bit about my experiences with former military training and railway work and talking French he suddenly said 'all right go and get your kit see the medical officer and be back in uniform on Tuesday next'. I was then placed in the orderly's room, where I had to fill in some forms about next of kin, paid 8d for an identification disc and was told what kit to get. I was asked 'what religion?' I was a bit taken aback at this in the middle if all sorts of matter of facts questions about kit and so I began to stumble a bit 'Oh put him down as C. of E. said the abrupt orderly 'that covers a multitude of sins'. Then I saw the doctor who passed me like a bird.

He wrote excitedly to his Bonne Mama [9], *This is to tell you that to my great delight I am at last entered in the army.*

He told his father, *The bird is caught and behold I am in the British army.*

Alec went immediately to Nicholls of Regent Street to buy equipment which cost £47, including field glasses, a sword and revolver. The uniform was to be ready by the following Monday. The whole experience elevated Alec's flagging spirits.

Isn't it glorious I am more bucked with life than I have felt for months and months? I

The suddenly achieved responsibility Alec in uniform at Higher Faugan
Private Collection

don't feel quite sober for I am so bucked. The suddenly achieved responsibility makes me feel already five years older. He was 22.

Despite his earlier misgivings, Stanhope drew a sense of pride from his son's actions:

Full of pride at the decision Alec has taken. He is busy buying his uniform. I am thinking a great deal about it all, but more and more feel it is the best thing that could have happened. How proud he will be…I am sure you will join with me in the prayer that God may bless him and keep him in safety in his new life. We know that he will do his duty and acquit himself like a man.

Alec was, as ever, concerned about his appearance, but was delighted to be in uniform, even though it took time to get used to its foibles:

The uniform is a great success and is voted tres chic by the ladies of the house, but I had fearful difficulty to get into all the little straps and buckles. The boots are not yet ready which is a great nuisance. Some of the straps fairly beat me, and I rather resembled George Grass struggling into the pantomime costume on the stage. I think however that they are sword straps which of course I don't need.

On April 28 he travelled to Longmoor Camp in Hampshire where he was to begin initial training.

Full of anticipation and excitement the young officer was soon relishing every aspect of his new life:

R.E Mess,

Longmoor Camp, Hants.

Have just arrived to find a topping place in the pine woods country above East Liss. They are all exceedingly decent chaps and I have settled in in great style though I don't think yet my military training has advanced far yet. There is but a great deal I <u>can</u> train for here for its evident I have been caught for a pretty soft job.

There was just one dark shadow over the bright horizon. Alec knew he would be sent out to France within days:

I hope he (Stanhope) won't be very upset at the prospect of me going out at once. If that is so he must realise that at any rate I shall not get to the front for ages and even then the MFO and other transport offices are not really on the front line.'

Knowing the imminent departure for the continent might distress his father, Alec was keen to arrange a family reunion. Soon after arriving at Longmoor he sent several wires and wrote three letters. Interestingly he takes full control of every

Alec in his school cap, Stanhope Forbes (1904)
Penlee House Gallery House and Museum, bequest of Dr Eric Richards
© The Artist's Estate

Alec in Whites, Elizabeth Forbes.
Private Collection

***My Little Friend and Comrade*'**(Elizabeth Forbes)
Alec reading 'King Arthur's Wood', Elizabeth Forbes. Private Collection

never enjoyed a book more and yet I have never been so sad and never so excited' (Alec)

Alec Reading, Elizabeth Forbes. Private Collection

The Half Holiday (Alec home from school), Elizabeth Forbes
Private Collection

*He admonished me to be careful about the fit of the clothes which he thought I had a
tendency to make too loose and artistic*
2nd Lt. William Alexander Stanhope Forbes D.C.L.I. Stanhope Forbes
Courtesy of Cornwall's Regimental Museum, Bodmin

The Sancreed memorial,
designed by Stanhope
Forbes and based on his
painting

*Words fail me to express how
very deeply grateful I am for this
charming Gift* (Stanhope)

The stained glass window
commissioned by the Architects
Association

detail of the plan, lessening any anxiety for his father:

R.E. Mess,

Longmoor Camp, Hants.

If you came up to town on Saturday you are to motor down to see me on Sunday as this will be your last chance.

The brief visit was a great success. Stanhope and Maudie were delighted to see him in uniform:

when I caught sight of a well-known figure coming along walking very familiarly swinging his cane. He really does look awfully nice. I am glad to say I found him very well and fat. [(9)]

After the visit Stanhope recorded:

I have spent some delightful hours with dearest Alec. He is as happy as it is possible to be. It is quite probable he will start for France in a few days and he was so pleased to see me too. I need to tell you how proud I felt when I saw the young lieutenant looking perfectly stunning in his khaki. [(10)]

Alec was soon delighting in the novelty of military life:

May 3 1915

It's all tremendously interesting as being a sort of complete 'reverse engines' of all that I have hitherto done since Bedales.

May 5

I was attached to the orderly officer which means going around with him to turn out the guard, inspect three drunken prisoners, see that the canteen and mess rooms are clean and suchlike police jobs.

Typically Alec took every aspect of his training seriously. Ever-conscious of his personal shortcomings, he made every effort to present himself as a professional officer. On May 5 he recorded:

My chief trouble is enunciating words of command – I also want any useful handbook on salutes – grades of officers – formations of company battalions etc. words of command for a squad commander marching through a town. I went off to a lonely part of the moors with my drill book to yell commands to the elements as this is the best way to develop a parade voice.

Alec remained at Longmoor for longer than he expected, though his initial training had taken just a few weeks.

Something about it makes me afraid (Mrs Lionel Birch)

'On the Other side of the Stile was a whole new world', Elizabeth Forbes. An illustration from 'King Arthur's Wood' (1904)

Alec was the model for the character 'Myles'

Private Collection

5

On the Other Side of the Stile [11]

Alec embarked for Le Havre on May 11. There he received two inoculations. He stayed at the Grande Hotel Moderne and was pleased to record that 'King George' was to pay 6 francs towards the 11 francs bill. He was greatly impressed by what he observed as he walked back to his hotel on May 12:

> I passed a quay where an English yeomanry regiment was resting, kit and men all lying in heaps. I don't suppose I shall ever have again so fine a spectacle of the Expeditionary Force.

The 'Tommies' were singing *Tipperary* which, Alec commented, had become *that worn out ditty.*

Later that day he travelled by rail to Abbeville; the journey took thirteen hours. He described:

> 150 miles of glorious Normandy countryside on a priceless day on a perfectly heavenly ride.

From the comfort of his first-class compartment, of which he was the sole occupant, he could hear *Sister Susie's Sewing Shirts for Soldiers* being sung by Tommies further down the train.

On reaching the office at the 5th Division Railhead he began the task of familiarising himself with his new job with characteristic enthusiasm and optimism:

> The job promises to be quite decent. I spent the morning being initiated into the mysteries of rewarding work — its really going to be a most interesting work all the goods which come on one section to the M.F.O. attached to each army corps and all the kits etc. of killed and wounded officers are sent back by him to the depot here and so back to England. We also have the job of catching all the contraband which is sent back to England by officers and men possessed of a twisted sense of humour. For instance a certain lady residing at some Oxfordshire manor was about to receive a very fine old crucifix. Another Tommy was sending back an unfired grenade.

Alec was soon acknowledging his good fortune in receiving such an interesting posting:

> Believe me I appreciate it as such a privilege that I have be allowed job at the headquarters I.G.C. [(12)]. Life is such a round of song and gaiety. It's rather interesting to reflect that while one joined the army expecting to be bored to extinction, it has so far turned out and still continues to be the hugest joke and very best time I've ever had. Everything is absorbingly interesting. I saw the supply train into the station about 8.45 a.m. Till it comes there is nothing more to do.

On the same day he attempted to write a description of what he had seen. Seeing the horrors of the war-torn landscape, he is still able to show a keen artistic awareness of colour and the natural world:

> I wish I could now set to and write a journalistic account of a countryside laid desolate by the Huns sword; of shrapnel bursting everywhere and fearful din. As it is all the country is smiling and lovely and all the young poplars breaking into leaf are a sheen of copper gold.

> All one can see are the regiments resting by the roadside here and there a big grave where probably 50 men lie together, the long long lines of ammunition wagons and London motor busses 'going up' and 'coming down', trains very slowly steaming into the little railhead station Stations with their cargo of cannon fodder or fodder for them, our aeroplanes (sic) hovering over, one can usually count six or so in the sky at once, and lastly 8 miles away one hears the guns.

One of his jobs was to supervise the forwarding of newspapers for the Front, sorting them into bundles for various units, after taking copies of the *Daily Telegraph* and the *Daily Mirror* for themselves. During this first week of initiation he familiarised himself with the railheads, the termini where goods were detrained before being taken to the front, and described 'joy rides' on postal lorries and travelling two miles on an old London motorbus now painted grey with its windows boarded up. Though far from the front lines there were constant reminders of what was happening there. Alec watched as casualties passed through on their way home:

> The gas cases look so frightful, and the others their wounds bleed so profusely that all the lint and wool bandages in which the poor things are swathed are soaked before they get home.

and heard:

> All day the big guns have been booming in the far distance. Every now and then things in the office rattle and the ground shakes.

Within days he persuaded a fellow officer to take him closer to the Front:

So after lunch today Pauling took me for a long walk. We went over the frontier into Belgium, and up a hill which in these parts is a considerable eminence commanding an immense view of enemy territory – to over – we could see the city of – Oh! Mr censor you did think to catch me that time – no, no names. When I asked for Hill 60 he pointed it out among the far distant undulations. Pauling laughed at me for being so impressed (All letters from France were censored - locations, dates and unit details were not allowed).

On 23 May Alec was sent to the 5th Corps railhead, where he was to be A.M.F.O.,

I have certainly fallen on my feet this time.

He asked the family to send out some essential supplies:

I shall be very pleased if you could send me some (now don't go reading this aloud at a family party!)

Aperient – Enos for example

Some toilet paper – for sanitary arrangements here are very crude

Some soaps

Punch *please – all other papers I can get here.*

Drawing implements – a block, india rubber, paint box and brushes (pencils I have) all of which you will find in my room.

Some small and cheap editions of books – for I find I have plenty of time to read I should like if possible Tess of the D'Urbervilles *some G K Chesterton –* Romany Rye *or some of William Morris prose – I expect you can get them in the cheap editions I have no fixed choice.*

Also please a toothbrush and some sweets – lemon acidulated drops or some sucky sweets – cigarettes I can always get free.

Life in the officers' mess was comfortable and entertaining. Alec described one meal, served by waiters in khaki, which included soup, asparagus, a joint of meat, new potatoes, apple pie, jelly, trifle and cigars. As they ate the waiters had placed light music on an excellent gramophone set on a marble base.

Alec commented, *they talk of the hardship of the front!*

He was even able to take a bath and bathe in the river:

I can assure you that the canvas bath is used daily. I've had a free afternoon spent by the reedy banks of the Somme – and also in it – for I had a delightful bathe with tea at a jolly cafe by the water's edge reading Eugenie Grandet

and enjoy one of this favourite pastimes: fishing:

Last night I had another jolly exped up the river. We mess at 7 – so taking into consideration the time it takes to get up the stream – it leaves parlous little time for real work on the water. But I really believe half the beauty of fishing is the tender manipulation of rod and line under trees and over bushes thro reeds – adding to that the wonderful charm of the river scenery – it's very enjoyable even with no fish in sight. Still you know I am not adept at the fly and will probably have to lapse to the humble worm which did last week at any rate bring me moderate luck. I shall be delighted to receive the rod and am glad to hear that a saffron cake is drifting this way too.

The day before yesterday four of us started out with bamboo rods and the most appalling tackle in a huge punt on a lovely Harpignies lake.

On the 25 May Alec described his delight in using a new form of transport,

I had a capital day yesterday. As I have told you I am now in possession of one of King George's motorbikes. I had a couple of lessons at my last railhead and so started off gaily yesterday to visit two other stations that I look after. It's a perfectly delightful way of getting about – no peddling or trouble at all. I have been into the ditch twice as I think I mentioned in my last letter.

Stanhope was wary of the acquisition:

Higher Faugan

28 May 1915

Dearest Alec

I hope you keep well yourself old chap. Glad you like that beastly old byke (sic) of course it must be a jolly way of gadding about and I daresay you will learn to hop off safely when it tumbles over.

It seems Stanhope's fears were justified. One of Alec's friends, a subaltern named simply Glyn [13] had set off on a new motor bike. As he set off Alec shouted out, *Don't come off'*, to which Glyn replied, *'I'm sure I'll kill myself'*. *'He had a bad spill six miles out of town and died three hours later.*

Alec quickly got over the loss of his friend and was soon writing of pleasant diversions amidst the ruins of war torn Northern France. For his 22nd birthday, on May 26th, Maudie and Stanhope sent him a hamper from Fortnum and Masons and he chose to share its contents with his fellow-officers and three nurses:

> Yesterday the great event of the day was a tea party. The billet consists of three of us so we asked three very charming nurses from the ambulance train, three damsels rather in the style of my 'nanna' of the neck operation. They giggled and wriggled and everybody looked profoundly terrified. How killing boys and girls can be ensemble if they haven't received a Bedales training. (I always am in a panic in spite of Bedales) but we managed to enjoy ourselves very much and Maudie's chocolates disappeared altogether.

There were also the usual temptations for serving soldiers:

> Ladies – very chic and sweet – some as yet 'unattached' to the Staff. One reminded me of that jolly little party we saw dancing in Andalusian <u>male</u> peasant costume on a table in a Tangiers café. She had the most charming way of signalling – talking with a toothpick. Now I've heard of ladies in the old times flirting across the room with fans or bouquets – But a toothpick is really the most modern and if wielded deftly can be most charming. I was just beginning to reply and comprehend with cigarette code when I beheld the sternly cynical eye of a British Major fixed upon me – whereat I froze into the rigidity – worthy of Lord Kitchener's most earnest disciple. One can be court marshalled if one is seen going on joyrides with ladies – isn't that un-Bedalian.

After telling his fellow-officers about the women he had observed, they were quick to mock him with the threat of court marshal and bestowing on him the title 'O. C. Flappers'.

Alec evidently enjoyed the companionship of women. He was proud to boast of his confidence in their company and his enlightened attitude towards female suffrage, *I got into fearful hot water the other day on the subject of women's suffrage, and pacifism hasn't got a chance.*

Despite all the delightful distractions the tedium of walking round goods yards carrying a clipboard was beginning to prove unbearable for a young man thirsty for more meaningful work. His job was for 'heroes' who had returned wounded from the front or for older men unable to contribute to the active war: real railway men. He concluded, *in the forwarding work I still feel no more in the war than when I was at home.*

He soon realised that the role he was to play was unlikely to prove demanding:

15 May

I am frankly extraneous. There doesn't seem to be a great deal in this game. As far as I can see I am out here for a thorough old slack. All the men I have met say that they have never slacked so much in their lives. Certainly I've never enjoyed myself so much. As far as serving ones 'King and Country' has consisted in unmitigated good time.

By June 6 Alec was unable to conceal a contempt for the easy life he was leading:

Life is all too easy..

This is a fearfully slack job.

The novelty of railhead work behind the front is apt to wear off.

When I compare it with last summer's swot at architecture this does seem such a bloomin holiday.

He recognised that he had never coped well with idleness, *I am never very stoical if there isn't a great deal of work to do.*

Furthermore, the attitude of some of his brother officers appalled him, *Bachelors, very independent and irresponsible to whom the war is rather a joke.*

He was also aware that his railhead work would soon come to an end. By the middle of July he had already made his feelings about a possible transfer to a front line regiment clear. Stanhope responded by writing his son a 'sermon' on the subject and Alec was keen to put his father's mind at ease, though he was hiding the truth, *I am very content with plenty to do.*

But by the 24 July Alec was once again displaying his discontent, writing of, *This appalling little job* and adding *this is such a menial job.*

On 25 July 1915 he was in despair and was growing impatient:

This present is too intolerable a farce – altogether it's far too jolly and sociable to suit my aspiring mind and since as I said yesterday its now too late for me to be trained for the trenches I am certainly anxious to have a shot at a more regimental job than is the Railway Transport Establishment. You must realise that we have never had so great a chance to do our utmost and this life here make a chance to do our utmost – and this life here makes me glow with shame when I think how very far from being my utmost it is. So don't be unhappy and worry if I get myself into a regiment. There are stacks of officers ahead of me. I feel sure you need not worry about my chances of getting to the front. The fates seem opposed to that!

He offered his father some consolation in the event of a transfer, suggesting that a move to a front-line regiment would mean a return to England for several months of training. For Stanhope the hope might also have been that by the time his son was trained the conflict might have come to an end. Stanhope responded:

You can guess I do not contemplate the idea of your going with the infantry without grave concern, though of course the prospect of having you in England is an attraction.

Despite the frustrations he experienced it was clear Alec earned the respect of his fellow-officers and performed his duties efficiently. He had developed a good relationship with his commanding officer, who sought to encourage him to remain with the RTE:

He (Captain Simpson) told me again yesterday that although I am only a supernumerary on his staff he'd be quite willing for me to remain. So you see I am always immensely grateful to you for this commission which I owe entirely to you. I only greatly wish that I had some railway experience to entitle me to remain in the RTE.

Alec was soon working on what he described in a letter to his father as a 'scheme', *I am so tempted by the D.C.L.I. scheme – you could work that! I bet it would allow me to go down there and months of training*

In the same letter he wrote:

I wonder what are the latest developments in the official correspondence between Higher Faugan and 189 Maida Vale re the 'Son of the firm'. I am so sorry if I am going to cause worriment, but I think you do all take a premature view of the situation if you assume I am in for desperate things. I do think its incumbent in my position for me to do more than handle parcels and as for the horrors of war' well I don't yet even know my squad drills, so I can't get to the Front yet. I am sure Uncle Willy will settle down and eventually accept the new scheme and you will surely be prouder of me in a regiment than in a parcels office. You see Dad it may all sound vague and far away when you are in Cornwall, but reflect that I am now well in khaki and it is the most natural thing in the world to change from the administrative to the executive branch of the army.

Stanhope pleaded with his son to accept his position, telling him he was *doing his bit* and should be content, but it was all to no avail. Alec was determined to act and wrote to his father on the 9 August:

I must confess I am still moving heaven and earth to get moved into some sort of Infantry scheme. Now I believe they are raising a new battalion of the D.C.L.I. in Cornwall. If you would write to Lt Col Harvey D.S.O. o/c Depot D.C.L.I. Bodmin.

On 16 August he confirmed:

<u>I must admit that a correspondence is going forward with a view to a transfer to some infantry show</u> and I am much bitten by the chances of getting into a new battalion of the DCLI. If dad would write to Col Harvey OC depot Bodmin he could do it in a moment I am sure.

There were those who sought to dissuade Alec from following the course of action. Harry Jacob [14], one of Alec's A.A. pals, wrote on August 21:

Dudmans Dock Grove Street Deptford

My dear old William

Thank your stars old dear you are out of it and keep out of it, its hell this is unpatriotic I know but there you are, as for being 'little willyish' that is of course just BALLS. It makes me so wretched to think of all my and your carefully thought of plans come to nothing, but if I come out of this alright we must go together as 'per arranged' the only thing is how long will it last.

A Newlyn friend and son of the artist Norman Garstin, Denys, recalled a meeting he had with Alec at the time [15]:

It is hard at this time to remember dates and details but it was the end of June or beginning of July 1915. I was stationed near Hazebruck and he was up at Bjursnight, in the Belgium frontier, so we wrote and met twice at Hazebruck. It was ripping meeting him but in a way I hated it. He was so full of apology for his safer work and when at lunch we all, add officers from a dozen regiments, told yarn after yarn of the fighting along the line, Alec was resolving all the time to get somehow into the common danger. He told me so and I tried to dissuade him, but I felt that he wasn't happy in what he called the work of an embusque (shirker). It was all rot as his work was as necessary as any of ours, but Alec wasn't the fellow to take any excuse for avoiding danger. And that was almost all we talked about sitting on the sunny terrace of the Hazebruck café. But once I said something about people seeing this war only as a form of madness, and at once he soared away into the idealism of it all, his idealism of it.

Sir William Forbes, who had been so central in securing a safe job for Alec, also sought to discourage Alec:

I have received a rather perplexing note from Uncle Willy, who seems very bored at my move into infantry – But, dear daddalorums, I do so deeply think I've had enough of parcels and goods traffic and am so anxious to be training in England for some job with more in it. He very charmingly backs you up and urges me to stay on the lines of communication. Well you know I would stick at it if I thought I was really doing any good here.

You evidently all feel that if I leave this show I am bound for the trenches in a very short time – I am sure I shall never be there, and its only my silly egotism that makes me want to be able to say that I am in some regiment that makes me leave this RTE. How can I tell Uncle Willy who so absolutely lives in his railways that I cannot care for this work. He is evidently under the impression that I am giving up a splendid job to drop from £300 to £170 a year – but as you and I do seem to so always think alike, I leave it to your intuition and your responsive mind to realise all the little reasons that make me want to serve my country better than by handling parcels.

Most of the family remained opposed to any transfer. But Alec was adamant and believed they would soon come to accept the decision:

August 16

My dear Uncle Willy

I was so sorry when I got your letter this morning to learn that you all are so opposed to my transfer to Infantry. But you know I have discussed this with Dad for some time in my letters and though I don't for a moment maintain that he approves – he knows my wishes clearly enough, and I think that once I am training in England he will settle down to the idea.

The family, guided by Uncle Willy, now attempted to frustrate Alec's plans by securing medical advice which would establish that he was physically unfit for front line service. Only May Forbes seemed ready to dispel the doubts they raised. Her strong condemnation of the family wishes must have strengthened Alec's resolve:

Aug 19 1915

How tiresome the family can be and un-understanding! Such very good kind 'fatherly' intentions but no soul in them. Wasn't brought up at Bedales – Of course life teaches us each differently and you and I have learnt and am learning how jolly it is to have something to give that really costs something. We get lots of fun during the giving and we shan't be happy if we don't get our fun in our own way. Write very cheerfully about anything you can, mention briefly casually that you have made up your mind to do what you think is your duty. The army people will understand all right, and in the end the family will respect you all the more. Of course be sure your body is fit enough to make a decent officer! It would be better to be a good bottle washer with a feeble body than a bad officer, no nerve etc. because you were not physically fit! Isn't there a competent understanding sort of doctor you can confide in out there!

It is easy to feel shocked by May's references to *fun* as she seeks to assist Alec on his way to the trenches. She, like most who looked on from home, had little or no concept of what he would face on the front line. In a later letter May added:

Well it is a nuisance for you, but I hope very much you will have got the doctor on your side by quite plainly and simply putting your case and the family's, and telling him you see through their little manoeuvres and ask him to treat you as a man. The real truth after a sound examination though if he doesn't consider you fit you must play through the family too and just do the best in your present job. Of course you are much too sensible to grizzle if you don't get your own way if it is done fairly and squarely but it is very trying to feel there is a sort of backdoor game going on, and pleasing Cousin Willy comes before helping you to do the best in the war you can! There are my sentiments! Write and tell if anything fresh happens. Act calmly and strongly is my advice.

On August 21 Alec had been granted a few days leave. He was to cross to England by the night boat and would sleep at the Grosvenor before catching the *Cornish Riviera* train on Monday.

Alec finally got his way. During the five days in Newlyn he slipped away one morning and travelled to Bodmin to the H.Q. of the Duke of Cornwall's Light Infantry and applied to join the regiment. At the end of his leave Stanhope accompanied his son on the night train from Penzance to London. Stanhope later recorded the journey and his shock on observing the scene at Victoria:

Night train 29th August 1915. We curled up after Plymouth in our sleeping berths and had a good night, the last one I was to spend with my dear son in this way we had so often enjoyed together. At Victoria drunkenness among soldiers wives were deplorable some scandalous things to be seen. I remember clasping my dear boys hand as he got into his carriage, and standing there whilst the train moved off. May and Louise came after me, and I parted from them and spent an hour alone walking across the park.

By August 31, just four months after he had acquired his commission in the R.T.E., Alec secured a transfer and was ready to join the 'real' war. He remained acutely aware of his father's concerns:

Heedless of the pain it might give you. You must now feel that I shall be more directly in the war even though I may never see the front and you must feel that I shall be doing more for this terrible crisis – than playing for safety behind the lines.

Soon after his brief return to France he wrote:

Herewith once more kicking up my heels, and if it wasn't for the prospect of imminent healthier and more strenuous work, I should be feeling very much down as the aftermath of leave. But how glorious it was while it lasted. 5 days of perfect weather and enjoyment that now remains like 5 very bright gems of memory. Yes indeed. I do consider it's an escape to run from these trucks and trains and everyone says how lucky I am to have the prospect of England before me.

Stanhope had now come to accept his son's decision and expressed regret for the effort he had made to dissuade him. He knew his intervention must have been tiresome, *Daddalorums, who has been a nuisance to you and impeded your progress.*

On September 13 1915 Alec sent a telegram to his father:

Reported War Office passed fit told to wait further orders so arriving Newlyn 5p.m. tomorrow.

6

Seeking the Common Danger

Spurning the advice and wishes of family and friends, Alec had rejected the safety of railway work and chosen a course which would take him to the heart of bloody conflict. He knew that he was physically and mentally ill-suited to the role of a professional soldier, *Although army life is rather jolly I shall have no difficulty in getting back to paints.*

On collecting his pistol and sword he declared they were not really his sort of thing, *I don't think I need a sword; a good fountain pen will be more my form, so will go on the old assumption that the pen is mightier than the sword etc.* (April 23 1915)

In a letter to Cousin May he included a caricature of himself in uniform, adding his own admission that he felt the singular ineptitude of the Kitchener poster. Anxiety about his appearance extended to the uniform he wore:

> *I have a new cap, it fits me which is one detail the old one failed in – it is really very chic – the new soft and pliant khaki type, and after ten weeks in the army (! I don't think) I feel I can sport it better. In any case I look less of a geyser than I did in that beastly great big thing Nicholls sent me out with. I now feel so opulent and staffy.*

The portrait Stanhope painted of him in uniform does not lie. Though Alec appealed to his father to put aside artistic considerations and paint his uniform tight and sharp. (Stanhope wrote, *I remember how he admonished me to be careful about the fit of the clothes which he thought I had a tendency to make too loose and artistic*). The completed portrait shows a brave and committed 'amateur' drawn into the world of professional soldiering.

After his arrival in France he had been 'mocked' by French girls who, on seeing him in uniform, commented, *Quel drole de petit officier'*. Throughout his training and service Alec had been dogged by self-doubt and fears that he lacked the physical and mental qualities required to lead men. Like his father he had a quiet manner of speaking and a slight physical frame. During his first week of training at Longmoor he had walked the surrounding hills practising giving orders and developing parade ground voice:

Alec's caricature of himself
in uniform

Private Collection

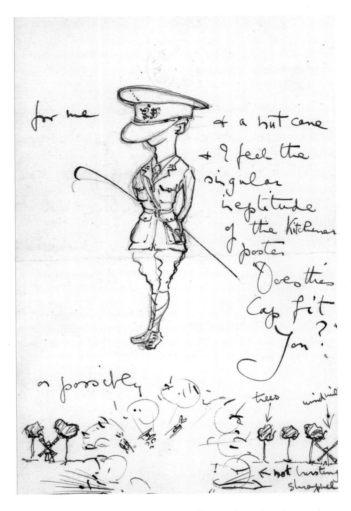

I have not of course had much opportunity of yelling orders – but it has happened once or twice since I have been here and I must confess at first to the 'afraid of his own voice stage' through which great many newly-gazetted officers have to go I expect! I am getting over it now and can look the 100 pair of eyes in the face though at first you want the ground to swallow you up.

Alec was certainly not an insensitive warmonger. He was revolted by the futility of the conflict, *It makes me curse with fury this dammed carnival of war.*

Struck by the destruction of old churches he exclaimed, *It only makes me ache for the end of the war.*

On hearing of the death of a fellow architectural student, Bernard Walsh, he lamented, *You know my views on art and architecture. I can't tell now how terrible it is that all the talent and genius of that art should be thrown into the furnace of the war.*

One strong motivation for Alec stemmed from the pride he felt in his inherited French blood. Stanhope commented, *Don't forget to tell them that you have a little French blood in your veins and that some of your ancestors come from Abbeville. We used to call Bonne Mama the Duchess of Abbeville.*

The Germans had invaded a country he more or less considered to be his second home. *Perhaps its dear old Bonne Maman's blood which makes me feel the honourable necessity of going ahead and if I am prevented I shall feel that we didn't come up to scratch at this crisis.*

But Alec wasn't a 'blind patriot' who was simply responding to anti-German propaganda, which included rumours that the Germans were raping French women, crucifying captured soldiers and murdering children. This was a sensitive, intelligent young man who could not share the ecstatic joy of those who delighted in seeing men suffering pain and humiliation. Whilst working at the railhead he encountered a train loaded with wounded German soldiers. An N.C.O. told him, '*Well sir they was a changing them just now and as they were a liftin one out on the platform blessed if he didn't drop dead. Oh it was a lovely sight*'.

Alec responded by saying he preferred to miss such *lovely sights.*

He, like many others, may have been unable to fully comprehend the horrors he would face if he was posted to the Front line. He often presented a purely aesthetic appreciation of what he observed.

On 17 May 1915 he described:

The whirr and screech and boom with puffs of sharp white smoke contrasting with the hazy blue of the clouds behind as if you flicked some Chinese white solid on to a sketch painted in pale blues and yellows in wash – this was German shrapnel, and it excited me terribly to see and hear it all for the first time.

On the 25 May 1915 he once again described events through the eyes of an artist:

> *My great delight was the sight of a German plane being peppered by our anti-aircraft guns. It was a beautiful sight for at sunset the bursting shrapnel look like little flecks of gold.*

Yet, despite an apparent lack of self-confidence and motivation, Alec's education had from an early age been taught him to step up to every challenge. Like most young officers he had yet to gain any experience of the real world and had only the lessons he had been taught as a boy to fall back on. The young officers who led their men out of the trenches during the First World War were the sons of a society which glorified self-sacrifice and condemned moral and physical weakness. Young boys like Alec had read stories of daring and adventure which set out to instil a sense of duty and honour in impressionable young minds. Cautionary tales, such as *Eric or Little by Little* (1858), *Tom Brown's Schooldays* (1857) and *The Hill* (1905), celebrated the heroic spirit and highlighted the evils of cowardice, bullying, caddishness and sexual immorality. They expounded the great virtue of displaying *firm chinned loyalties and unswerving devotion to one's gentlemanly code of ethics.*

In his response to the war Alec frequently referred to the education he had received at Bedales. It had left an indelible mark on his character. He wrote an account of a chance meeting with an old school friend:

Fort Purbrook

14 October 1915,

I haven't seen Harry Jacob again but at a concert at Southsea on Sunday I ran into Hardy – a chap who used to be in my dormitory at Bedales – He is quartered in Portsmouth in the Oxford and Bucks light infantry – he came up to see me on Tuesday and last night. I dined with him and we went to a very rotten music hall which with our lofty aesthetics training we neither approved nor enjoyed. But we jawed lengthily upon the effect of Bedales and the army and came to the sage conclusion that rather than the two being antagonistic the one is an excellent training ground for the other. Bedales makes one energetic and disciplined and after all that's what one needs in Kitchener's army rather than swank and nuttiness. I was amused at his mess to find him very Bedalian in his tastes – doesn't drink or smoke at all. He left Bedales about a year ago and then went to Sandhurst for he is making the army his career' we are going to do a weekend at Bedales together as soon as possible.

Alec was proud of the stance taken by his old school on militarism. Badley, the Headmaster was, *turning the top form into an OTC and making all of his staff drill – Isn't that capital.*

On the 14 November 1915 he wrote of a visit to his old school and the staff:

The staff now is nearly all female except for the old stagers and one dreadful man who wont enlist because he has conscientious objections – so I spread sedition in the school in respect of him but was informed roundly by one youngster – 'Oh! But nobody listens to old Roper – he's quite a washout' I was relieved.

On another visit he recorded,

Yesterday my Bedales tea party came off splendidly – I found Ivy Escapp – the ideal wife of a most ripping naval man – they make a most delightful and amusing couple. The other Bedales girls were so ripping too and made out that all the very excellent homemade cakes were baked that morning in my honour. That by the way is probably why little May is unhappy today (Alec often referred to the state of his 'tummy'. For some reason he nicknamed his tummy 'My Little May' when he corresponded : *My Little May doesn't like the cold, she has caught a chill and grumbles fearfully at this military ardour; I haven't bathed for two days because it's very much colder here and little May has had a pique at all this strenuous exercise). We talked endlessly of Bedales people and the war. These girls had made out a roll of honour and find that 70% of the boys are serving excluding the foreigners of whom they have no news. Now as they were as an average 15% at least – we calculated (Russians and Dutch) in the school – the 70% is most extraordinarily high – Isn't it splendid!*

Alec's education and character led him to reject idleness. His energy and enthusiasm more than compensated for any lack of aggression. After an afternoon's expedition at Fort Purbrook he was to comment:

In this way one avoids a state of mind so prevalent among unfortunate subs. – utter boredom – personally if I didn't go in for these sort of excursions from time to time I should go dotty. Really the best thing in the world is to cultivate a sense or gift of interesting oneself. (9.1.16)

Unsurprisingly he was quick to condemn anyone who failed to meet his own standards. Above all he saved his fiercest criticism for those who were slackers, conscientious objectors and any who were unwilling to fight:

Still there is also the seamy side to life here – so many of the so-called officers continue to be slack and the most undisciplined set of rotters I have ever set eyes upon. It's perfectly disgraceful and I know of 3 who are on the edge of being cashiered. The majority I really do believe never intend to become efficient.

In another letter he continues to criticise the attitudes displayed by many of those with whom he worked, *Young slacker.*

His loyalty and sense of duty led him to condemn those who failed to join the colours, *Well I must say that people who are 'Too proud to fight' will some day find themselves rather more detached or isolated than they would care for themselves.*

Like any young man of his time Alec wished to make his family proud and was forever conscious of the image he projected to those he met when he was at home. On his first visits to Newlyn in uniform he had swaggered proudly around the village in khaki. Stanhope noted, *To be wearing anything else would be intolerable and he knew he could not raise his head high.*

Alec was not satisfied with simply being seen in a uniform, though few in Newlyn would have appreciated the distinction between a safe job and that of front line soldier. Alec was an idealist and like his parents, who demanded perfection in their own work, compromise was not an option. If he was to wear khaki, it must be in the uniform of an officer in a front-line regiment. He refused to hide behind the sham of wearing the uniform and doing a cushy safe job. Aware that the efforts of the family might provide a safe option, it was his conscience which would never allow him to take the easy path,

Whilst at the railway forwarding office he had been glowing with shame at not being seen to do his utmost. He was brutally honest about his motives:

25 July 1915

Pure swank you see and nothing altruistic in my argument. No big solid religious fervour and so forth but merely the sordid wish that you people at home can say he is in the 19th Blistershires.

In vain I try and persuade myself that some people have to serve in humble ways, but really I do feel that I can tackle something better than wandering about a yard with a white notebook.

Did Alec believe a transfer to the infantry would not see him thrown into the merciless carnage of the trenches? Throughout the correspondence relating to the transfer Alec persistently claimed that he would remain safely away from the Front:

You evidently all feel that if I leave this show I am bound for the trenches in a very short time – I am sure I shall never be there, and its only my silly egotism that makes me want to be able to say that I am in some regiment that makes me leave this RTE.

And:

There are stacks of officers ahead of me. I feel sure you need not worry about my chances of getting to the front. The fates seem opposed to that!

16 August

If I thought that I should be in the trenches in 6 weeks – believe me that I should be very chary of this transferal I can aspire to is to be one of a vast reserve of infantry subs who will never see the Front.

How much of this optimism was simply a deliberate attempt to calm the fears of the family? Whatever his declared thoughts were, it is difficult to believe that with all his talk of slackers and cowards, Alec's decision was not motivated by the hope that he might share the common danger with brother officers.

In correspondence with his cousin he readily entertains the possibility of serving on the front line. May sent Alec a gift which would prove invaluable if he really was heading for the darkness and gloom of the trenches.

Sept 1 1915

My dearest May

This is to formally thank you for the ripping watch which keeps such capital time – one might make a joke upon the theme of 'the watches of the night' and its certainly very amusing to be able to tell the time in bed. Query will it ever be used in darksome trenches?

Dear Maudie is so sweet and good and tends me so carefully (Alec)
I loved the boy so dearly (Maudie)

Alec with Stanhope, Maudie and Meg (the family dog) at Higher Faugan, 1916.
Penlee House Gallery & Museum Archive

7

The Making of an Infantry Officer

The transfer offered Stanhope an opportunity to spend many happy days with this son. Alec was to undertake his infantry training back in England. For the moment at least the worst attrition of the war would not pose any threat to his welfare. A further cause for celebration was the realisation that much of Alec's initial training would be based at Fort Purbrook in Hampshire. This would take Alec back to the area he had so enjoyed exploring whilst at school near Petersfield. He would also be close to Bolderswood, where relatives lived. There were months of happiness ahead; Stanhope was later to consider them to be the finest months he had enjoyed with his beloved Alec. He included a detailed account of the months which followed.

9 Sept On Thursday he writes what he tells me will be his last letter from the B.E.F. in active service. He is to cross on Saturday report to the War Office on Sunday and speaks of hoping to catch the night train to Cornwall. I have no further letter as on the 13th he writes from Mr Wilkinson's office to say that the War Office had accepted him and he had been given permission to go home for a week. With intense joy I am to expect him by the 5p.m. train.

For two weeks Maudie, Stanhope and Alec were able to enjoy precious time together. Stanhope describes excursions to Falmouth, Bosigran, Pendeen and attending church services at Sancreed.

On 28 September Alec reported for training at the Officers Training Company, Fort Purbrook. Shortly after his arrival he was in buoyant mood:

So far I have completely fallen in love with barrack life in a huge semi-medieval castle which I cannot get over, it is so delicious the old Victory lies below us surrounded by modern shipping of all sorts, navy grey predominantly.

He worked hard to overcome the weaknesses he so readily identified. He was still anxious to master the art of taking drill:

5 October 1915. Fort Purbrook

Some of us have an extra drill on our own from 5–6 and after mess sit around the fire in our room in our pyjamas and drill with matches on a table. I have all to learn!

The tedium of practice was punctuated by amusing incidents:

Oct 20 1915

Company drill

We had four unusually droll subalterns and were making more than passing fools of ourselves. Some kids watching at the edge of the parade ground called out,

'Come on Bill 'eres some soldiers drilling'

'Cor blimey They ain't soldiers they be Orficers!!'

The whole company roared with laughter.

Months later he was delighted to report that he had finally mastered the art of giving orders on the parade ground, *I got thorough the drill without making the usual numerous faux pas and mistakes that are so salient a feature of many subalterns' drill.*

Marksmanship though was an ongoing problem, *So far I haven't done particularly well and I really am no shot nor ever will be I think. Still it is fascinating and the long mornings on the range so very enjoyable .(12.4.16)*

He found one part of his training much more suited to his interest and skills, *Tactics and field sketching I love. The Colonel has been sending me out making field sketching discourse with avidity. I am so thankful to find my art training is of some use here.*

He found the drawing of range cards particularly satisfying, *It quite appeals to my aesthetic sense.*

There was also the unique bond of comradeship amongst all serving officers and soldiers which he greatly appreciated, *This sort of army bonhomie is very cheering, for certainly one does find more cheeriness and good nature in the army than anywhere else I think.*

By 30 October he was relieved to tell his father, *the exams are partly through now. I think I have done fairly well on the engineering and tactics papers*

As ever he maintained a positive and cheerful attitude during what must often have been a gruelling training regime for a young man with delicate health:

My dearest Dad

May wasn't able to have me at Bolderwood – she is away – and so I came over here and have spent the afternoon wandering round – watching drill and shooting and riding and gardening and so on.

At Purbrook this morning we began with a route march and then had an exam on general military knowledge – machine guns, law, tactics, musketry, interior economy and so on – I don't in the least know how I got on as far as marks are concerned but I wrote down a great and hope I passed. I haven't seen Colonel Fawkes lately though he very charmingly sent me a little card asking me to tea last week. Great honours. The best thing has been a machine gun course we have just begun. – it's going to be very interesting indeed.

I am thankful to say we do less drill now – we lie about more on the Downs carrying out imaginary attacks. Thanks for the tummy band – you will be amused to hear that it's going to be used for wrapping up the tummy of my revolver and for cleaning it!

Part of the time I was down on the range watching some very excellent shooting. Since then we have been making some toast over the library fire. I have just heard that John Russell is just off to Serbia – rather terrific for him isn't it! Well love to you all. Glad to hear the chickens are laying I haven't heard any news of Wee Wee lately but why is early morning parade (6.30) like her tail? Because its twirly (too early!)

On 18 December Alec began Christmas leave and went to visit his old school. Stanhope recalled, *On this day Alec wrote to me from Bedales School where he had gone expecting the usual Saturday night performance of the play King John. He found the school deserted as Mr Badley had decided it was simple to get rid of the School and had given the play a day or two earlier.*

On the following Monday Alec travelled home, arriving at Penzance on the 5p.m. train. The family spent a few quiet days together at the Faugan. Stanhope decided to begin a portrait of his son in uniform:

22 December I commenced in the evening the portrait of my son (22 Dec) in his uniform, as a 2ⁿᵈ Lieut. In the DCLI. I painted this by lamplight as I did not want to take up his time in the day. He was greatly interested in the proceedings and I remember how he admonished me to be careful about the fit of the clothes which he thought I had a tendency to make too loose and artistic. He sat on the Wednesday and again on the following night. We had a quiet evening. Whilst the family played cards my dear boy gave me a final sitting for his portrait.

Christmas Day Maudie Alec and I went together to Sancreed Church. They stayed on for the communion service whilst I waited on the road where they found me sheltering against a hedge from a shower of driving rain. I remember Alec being greatly concerned about my plight. Though I was really quite all right. In the afternoon we took a wagonette and drove to Lamorna and called on the Heaths and Birches with whom we took tea. The Birches had a little Christmas tea party on and he took us all up into the little room where this tree was lit up and the gifts distributed to the little ones.

*In the evening Mr Crowker and her son and Mrs Thorpe came to dinner. After it the Gotches looked in also the Misses Petty. And some other of my pupils. Ms Tonge Ms Fradgely and Ms Ashburn. We had music and dancing. **Alec was as happy as he could be.***

Alec, along with his cousin, left Penzance by train on 26 December.

Alec had been selected to attend a special course at the Clapham Grenade School. Though unhappy about the timing, which curtailed the Christmas leave, he was thrilled to have been chosen and relished every part of the new experience:

28/12/15

My dearest Dad

A line in greatest haste to say that the bombing course so far is great fun and <u>very</u> thrilling. All sorts of weird and mysterious 'Frightful' devices – you will be amused to hear that I have today been thro' a live cloud of gas. Thanks to the newest type of stink helmet we were using – we came out quite fit except for that curious feeling which one experiences on taking chloroform for an operation. Still one has no need to fear gas now and so there is no danger whatever. The bomb throwing is of course quite harmless. We were using a trench catapult all the morning for chucking bombs and in the afternoon a new toy which the public mustn't know about.

The crowd are very decent experienced men miles superior to that awful Purbrook crowd. They come from all parts. Inniskillens, Gordons (there are a great many kilts) and I am the only DCLI. The old major has really been a brick to send me here.

He wrote again on the 30 December:

This place continues to be vastly entertaining. The hours are from 10 to 1 and from 2 to 4 – not very strenuous you see. This morning we played (there is no other word for it) with some of the new bomb throwing devices and also carried out a bomb storming attack on some trenches – first rushing the trench and throwing in bombs at one end and then having 'captured' the trench – pursuing imaginary 'Boches' who fled in abject terror – up communications trenches and into their dugouts. – It's all most realistic. Rumour has it that there is to be another gas attack.

4p.m. have just come thro' a gas attack and beyond feeling rather headachy, am quite amused by it. We advanced throwing 'stick' bombs and then as this morning with the high explosives proceed to follow up the attack into the trench in my own fumes – hence the respirators! Now for tea for a faint smell of gas still pervades my lungs and clothes. Ever yours Alec.

Now Alec was keen to be posted to his regiment. Finally, on 1 March he left Fort Purbrook and joined D Company, 3rd Duke of Cornwall's Light Infantry at Golden Hill, Freshwater, on the Isle of Wight. He wrote:

Enfins – chez le regiment! Five of us left Purbrook yesterday morning and after buying various necessities and having a very good lunch in Southsea embarked with a huge stack of kit. The journey thro the island takes a fearful time! We fetched up at about 5 and plunged about in the rain looking for quarters. A new subaltern is always received at this regiment in a very casual way – Hullo, you rolled in from Purbrook? Poor blighter! How long you been there? 5 months! Great mercies – poor devil!

The first day has gone down very well. We have made our room most delightfully comfy, with arm chairs and a thick carpet and a fire going all day.

Shortly after his arrival he received some disparaging comments on the quality of his clothing, *Sergeant Seaman doesn't approve of my pants and vests, but he says my socks, knitted by Mabel, are very good indeed. He approved of my new trench coat and says that my old Burberry 'is fit to make 'im weep'.*

A week later he wrote:

3rd Duke of Cornwall's Light Infantry

Freshwater

8/3/16

My dearest Dad

Just a line today for there really isn't much news – an orderly officer duties came to all intents and purposes (as we thought) to an end at 11.30p.m. when we turn out the guard. I turned in at once and slept blissfully until a sudden shock and a great noise brought me back to this world – it was my servant very unceremoniously turning me out of bed, an all the hut in the passage outside was panic and confusion – 'the Zeps – Sir – Zeps sir – the alarms going and your to be on parade in 5 minutes!' – Half asleep with speed taught of old at Bedales when fire alarms were sounded I was bundled into my clothes and equipment and seizing a toothbrush and a revolver – I rushed forth to meet the airy Hun – incidentally a pun might be made on the motif – what is the difference between a Zep pilot and a French 'Poilu'

– answer – one is an airy Hun – and the other is a hairy 'un!) Still to proceed with our matters? I found everyone else similarly oddly equipped and servants officers (in Xmas tree rig – very fancy variety as it was 4 a.m.) and so all scrambling on parade just outside our hut , we met one of the Majors who told us – 'It's all right – it's not an official alarm – it's the real thing – there are two over us – the men are all paraded and everything is quiet so you people better go back to bed! – we turned back very joyfully and like Ajax – defied the heavenly (or hellish) flashes to do their worst. Today has been very tranquil – tomorrow we have another route march so I may not be able to get a letter off to you. Have just heard from John Russell – in the trenches at last – very cheery – poor little man. Yours Alec.

P.S. I really am proud of my Hun conundrum. It really was quite spontaneous.

The memory of his dear Mother remained at the forefront of his mind, Will you send out a wreath tomorrow to Sancreed for me? I hope Phillip can collect some primroses for it. They are in full bloom here. Love to all yours ever Alec.

Occasionally Alec found his life alongside fellow officers so time consuming that other important relationships suffered:

20/3/16

My dearest May

I am heartily sorry I messed up Saturday so effectually and probably put you out very much – for I gather you were on your way back to the Forest from London.

As it turned out the weekend here was a chapter of sins and tribulations. Owing to this draft going off on Saturday – there was a tremendous strafe in the mess on Friday night – we all got very drunk and wiled away the small hours with wine and song – as I pride myself on having inherited a good head for liquor I was able to be of the stretcher bearing party to conduct less fortunate ones to bed and so forth. Please forgive me – in future when I want to come to the New Forest I shall do so, irrespective of outside conditions. Now I must run to post this. With heaps of love Yours very penitent and still rather 'peckish' Alec

The only consolation is that in this wicked world if you must get on the trained list – please the adjutant.

My Little May doesn't like the cold, she has caught a chill and grumbles fearfully at this military ardour. I haven't bathed for two days because it's very much colder here and Little May has had a pique at all this strenuous exercise. That by the way is probably why little May is unhappy today.

He went on to give a humorous account of misunderstanding a predicament faced by one of his men:

> At the orderly room one morning the Sergeant Major said 'Pte Blank to see you sir— he wants 3 days leave'. So the soldier came in and said that he wanted leave because, 'My wife's expecting Sir, and it ain't mine neither!' His very cryptic expression was beyond me then for I hadn't had much experience. So to the horror of the Sergeant Major and everyone in the orderly room I said – 'Really – Yes, what is she expecting?'

> Now I have more experience and deal most tactfully with the conjugal triangles of Tommie's wife! Now I am off to dine with Lady Ritchie. I am not greatly looking forward to it for I have inherited from you a tendency to headaches after merry stunts.

On Friday morning the 28 April began Easter Leave and arrived at Newlyn by the night train. Once again the family were ble to enjoy a brief time together. Stanhope recalled:

> – after a rest and lunch we drove in the pony trap to Boscawen and had tea on the rocks.

> The following day we hired a wagonette and Maudie and Alec and I drove first to Penberth. Alec stopping on the road at Mrs Willie Bolitho's to see if Dennis Garstin had arrived – he was expected on leave and we had invited him to join but Mr Bolitho told Alec he wasn't coming till that night – after this we drove on.

> Lunched on the rocks on the east side of Penberth Cove. Alec tramped off cross country whilst Maudie and I drove to Porthgwarra. There we saw him waving to us as we neared the coastguard station. We then all three walked right round the coast past Nanjizel Bay to the Lands End where we had tea – sitting outside on their bench in front of the hotel. Thence home by Waymill? In the evening music some excellent violin solos from Misses Crooke and her friend Misses Parker – which Alec greatly enjoyed.

> 30 April

> On Sunday we went to Sancreed in the afternoon Edith Hunter and Molly Grant with Fryn Jesse came to tea also Rheam.

> 1 May.

> We drove to Bosigran Castle lunching near Ding Dong mine from there we walk across to Carn Galva. I think Meg and Sylvia (family dogs) both came with us and were very uncomfortable in the prickly gorse of this moorland walk. After lunch this

day we hired a motor and drove to St Ives where we had tea. This made us rather late for the Fortescues but we looked in and saw them and had a chat about Lionel. Another musical evening similar to the last.

3 May.

On the Wednesday morning Alec left by the 10 a.m. train.

Two days later Alec was able to reflect on the short leave spent at home, *The memory of the five days in Cornwall is very delightful and whatever happens to me in the next few weeks it will always be the hugest help to remember the last leave.*

In his journal Stanhope commented on how his son had enjoyed the break but was also prompted to mention his foreboding for the future:

He had not said very much to me on this subject, but about this time he was beginning to know that at any time he might receive orders to go to the Front. In a letter to Maudie before he came home he had told her it was very likely he would soon go but that he did not wish his Father to know as it would distress him. For that reason he was looking forward to this leave with particular interest – I recollect that he was exceptionally bright and happy all the time but we both knew what was impending.

Alec's 23rd birthday was unremarkable,

26 May 1916 (Friday)

I have had an odd birthday, the morning spent among the sand hills on the big long range running about like rabbits with wooden Germans in the distance, lugging about the beastly clumsy tripod and gun. I haven't bathed for two days because its much colder and 'little May' has had a pique at all this strenuous existence.

He was able to meet his father at Dorking on the following day. The training was becoming increasingly arduous and was talking its toll on Alec's physical well-being:

27 May.

I was not surprised to find him looking far from well when I met him at Dorking Station the next day. There was with him another 2nd Lieutenant in the train whom he introduced me to Charlie Lambert whom in afterwards met on the Isle of Wight. He was also going up to town for the weekend – I drove Alec back to the Halsteads and introduced him to them all and we sat and had tea on the lawn and afterwards. He Maudie Russell and I went for a walk to Boxhill passing by George Meredith's house which Alec knew from a little print at school. The next Sunday morning we also went off for a nice stroll in the opposite direction and came up to a fine place commanding a lovely view where we all sat on a bench and talked. We saw about a dozen or more aeroplanes fly over our heads, quite the largest fleet I have ever seen. We were also greatly excited by the continual rumble of guns in the distance. The sound though very faint was distinctly audible through for a time Maudie failed to catch it and Alec was vastly amused at my irritation because what I termed a beastly bird would result in drowning the faint sound by its singing it prevented Maudie from hearing it.

Alec continued to reassure his father that he would remain safe and far from the horrors of the front lines, even though he must have known the imminent danger he faced. Stanhope eagerly accepted his son's words:

I feel greatly confident and hopeful and all you tell me confirms this. It is not easy to write about it but you must know that I feel most proud and thankful and have complete confidence in your future. I will only ask you to accept, with regret, if you find that after all you are to be kept drilling your company a little longer and console yourself by thinking that your poor Daddalorums will have less cause for uneasiness. (Letter from Stanhope 6 July 1916)

By the 8 August Alec was still expressing the belief that it was unlikely he would be sent to the front in the immediate future. Following two hours digging trenches in the dark, from 10 to midnight, he recorded that two officers only just recovered from wounds were returning to France, *So that is perhaps all that will come of the DCLI casualties and we may be spared for some time yet.*

Like a man fighting against fate he had already arranged appointments to visit people on his safe return from the war. This included Carrie de Rouffignac, the wife of a local Master Mariner who had himself been the subject of a painting by Henry Tuke. Their home in Mousehole boasted a fine ceiling which Alec planned to draw when he returned to Newlyn.

There were other plans he dreamed of fulfilling. After months spent longing to be freed to play his part in the great conflict, he was now able to describe a more comfortable life he hoped he might one day enjoy. He longed to return to his beloved Cornwall and Higher Faugan where he might live in peace with Stanhope and Maudie:

I've just come from the Mess where everyone was talking of after the war – according to Public opinion – Wartime economies are nothing to Post war economies that will be enforced upon us, and if we have to turn to and work my own land and garden I shall not object! With some effort we could become a self-sufficient unit. Maudie would milk her cow and feed her chicks. I would garden – hew wood and fetch water – well you'd be G.O.C Utopia.

8

Be Good and Very Brave

Journey to the Trenches

On August 15 1916 a telegram [16] arrived at the Faugan, where Alec was enjoying a few days leave. He was busy cutting down a tree in the garden, *Please return at once. You must report to the embarkation commandant Southampton by 4 p.m. on Wednesday the 16th for B.E. France.*

The family had planned a day out riding and a car had been booked, *So the car which was to take us off riding – took me and kit to Station instead. Dad and Bonne Mama were capital and didn't allow me to see any distress. It was such a rush to get off, however, that there was not much time to think of anything.*

Though mindful of the distress his sudden departure might cause the family, Alec was thrilled to know he was at last on his way. Once settled on the train he wrote to May, *I feel full of beans and excitement, and yet I know that Faugan having to do the waiting job is a bit down at the mouth.*

He hoped he might somehow find an opportunity to meet her before departure:

> *If I find tomorrow that it will be best to go to Southampton via Brockenhurst I will wire you again – though I think it will be probably a large draft and we shall go to Cowes direct to Southampton. I will however try to cross by the 1.30 p.m. boat at Yarmouth arriving Brockenhurst 2.30. The 3 days leave were priceless.*

On August 16 Alec boarded a *very dirty* troopship, the S.S. *Archangel*, along with 500 officers, 500 N.C.O.s and a few other 'rank and file'. They sailed at 8.30. accompanied by cheering from two hospital ships and hailed by flags and handkerchiefs waved from boats full of holidaymakers.

Alec recorded:

> *It was a very moving sight to see all the Sergeants and Tommies in our ship being sent off by all those cheering crowds. – the whole Solent re-echoing to hackneyed*

airs of Tipperary – Auld Lang Syne – Keep the Home Fires Burning *and so on* –

The Solent, which had looked brilliant in the afternoon with the Aquitania *– white with a large red cross – shining in the sunshine, was now flashing with searchlights and the twinkle of our semaphore talking to our escort of T.B.Ds.*

Despite all the upheaval of the last two days and the daunting prospect of what lay ahead, Alec remained calm and single-mindedly maintained an orderly routine:

I undid my kit and went to bed even as far as pyjamas – but everyone else made the great mistake of remaining in their clothes – so I found them fagged in the morning. I got up at 5.30 and to my great surprise found we were moving in a leisurely way up a gorgeous river with huge chalk cliffs and thick woods full of jolly old chateaux as we had left the place I landed at last time I was in the B.E.F. at 3 a.m. and were going direct to the city where I was rather ill once upon a time.

Alec was delighted to be billeted in Rouen. Having reported to 2 Infantry Base Depot, unable or unwilling to rest, he was soon off to visit the Cathedral. In an effort to keep the men *busy* for the next few days there were *desultory* parades, from 9.30 to 12.30. For the rest of the time Alec was able to enjoy the delights of the old city:

What I really appreciate is looking up the Cathedral and churches in the evening. And as a rule we all foregather for drinks at a cinema and return to camp at 10 p.m.

After tea yesterday we climbed to the very top of the iron spire of the cathedral – very lovely view from the top but felt very dizzy getting up for it is all open iron work and the last 100 feet or so where the spire tapers away to nothing. There is only just room for the little winding staircase – the platform on the top is in a sort of cage – so it's quite safe 450 ft high.

They were, he concluded, all *largely happy* though he was concerned that his orderly at Freshwater had sent him out without towels and adequate socks:

So if Maudie would please send me 2 prs of strong and big socks and 3 small towels (really small ones) for I mustn't enlarge my kit much and on the other hand one can get them frequently cleaned.

Parcels should not be brown paper and string but should be sewn into rough cloth or canvas. that is the safest way. Also I find the chocolate Maudie gave me most capital and useful. Of course also some soap (Calver's Pure carbolic soap is the best for use out here) so long as I am here, there are all the comforts of civilization but I haven't the vaguest idea how long we shall be here – probably some days longer.

Letters home were now full of detailed notes on the sights to be enjoyed in Rouen.

The young officer appears to have succeeded in blocking out all thoughts of what lay ahead. Once again he was keen to distract his father from more pressing worries:

1st DCLI

No 4 Infantry Base dep of BEF France

Rouen

20.9.16

My dearest Dad

I now find that the place name of Rouen may be disclosed. That simplifies matters greatly for although it is inadmissible to tell you about the camps and hospitals – you will be amused to hear some more about my architectural excursions throughout the old city.

Do you remember the cathedral and the church of St Omer and St Maclan – the cathedral is rather bare inside and the glass has been much damaged – but there are some windows that are quite wonderful – some of the early 12th century type with small figured medallions and no tracery and others of the 16th century with big figure subjects which are quite in Brangwyn's manner. St Omer is better proportioned and a finer design but very cold for it has been 'well restored'. That is rebuilt to all intents. Last night we went to a Lena Ashwell concert in the gardens at the back of St Omer in the gardens a large choir of ASC tommies sang some oratorio pieces jolly well and the very large British audience seemed to like it well enough – but I enjoyed chiefly the pile of the old church in the twilight when the restored parts became merged in the gloom and I really think I've never seen a so finely balanced mass.

I hope you've noticed in the above address 1st DCLI. I have just heard that I am to be sent to the 1st Bn.. Isn't it hugely splendid. 6 of us go the 1st, the others to other battalion. It's very sad that we are to be split up and those not for the 1st Bn are very sick indeed.

You need not worry, for reasons you will guess, that I shall therefore see no scrapping for a very long time to come. Must write to Uncle Willy and May so cheer'oh – we are just off to the cathedral – I was detailed for church parade this morning so was unable to go down there this morning as I had intended.

On 21 August Alec prepared for the journey to the Front and wrote to say he was feeling very fit indeed and was hugely *bucked* at the prospect of serving with the Old 32nd. All, he reported, were in gay spirits. The weather was gorgeous. Once at the front Alec wrote an account of the journey from Rouen, admitting he and his fellow-subalterns had found the experience arduous:

1st DCLI

5th Division BEF France

23.8.16

My dearest Dad

En fins vous voice. We had the devil of a journey up from Rouen the old troop train being shunted and jolted about in the most merciless manner. On Tuesday morning we fetched up at a little wayside station filled with the usual RTOs AMFOs ASC etc officers. The typical railhead. After some coffee and the last of our rations we set off on the motor lorry supply column, which took us a very long run thro delightful … country with jolly little evidence of war except a few occasional rest billets with troops doing drill as on parade at home. Eventually we were landed at the dump, the place where the motor transport meets the horse transport.

We waited for about an hour and then a beast of an ASC officer arrived and said that we could not ride but must march – after seeing the kits on board we started off a short cut through the camp to the village where were the DCLI. We lost the way once and it took us about 2 hours to find this place on a piping hot day too! But the amazing thing about it was the absolutely peaceful and deserted nature of the countryside – no troops or airplanes – only the very very distant rumble of the guns and 4 rather footsore subalterns tramping over miles of golden corn on their way 'To the Front'. After we reached the Battalion we had lunch in a charming billet and shook ourselves down and went fast asleep – we hadn't slept or had breakfast during this long tramp – so you can imagine we were ready for it.

Today I have been on parade just as at Freshwater and the afternoon in an improvised range as usual in a cornfield. The Bn seems to be very fine indeed but everyone rather worn after their recent dusting. There is no one who was with the Bn. when it fought at Mons – and nearly everyone has only been here a few weeks or months at the outside. It is not strange in officers! So odd seeing that of the 14 of us who left Freshwater this day last week only 4 of us have joined the 1st the others all going to service Bn. I feel 'Some' proud I can tell 'ee'.

With typical sensitivity to the feelings of those who read his letters at Faugan he added:

Be good and v brave.

P.S. I forgot to tell you about the great send off the others of our draft gave us at Rouen. We had lunched very well indeed at the Angleterre. The depart is a wonderful sight – a train nearly a quarter mile long filled with all sorts of troops leaving the city wildly cheered by crowds of French people and above all the Angelic ladies of the YMCA who run the station canteens. If you ever have any pennies to spare give them to the YMCA canteen fund. The ripping ladies who run the show are too priceless and decent to us all. We were very sad to leave the others in our draft.

Sketch of Rouen follows. This is a scribble I did as the train was leaving Rouen station I had lunched all too well at the Angleterre – hence its shakiness!

As ever his mind never strayed far from his love of architecture, even if his weariness prevented him from enjoying it:

PPS I forgot to mention that on our journey in the middle of the night we passed the Parthenon of Gothic architecture (Amiens Cathedral). I did not see it – I was fast asleep.

After a brief time spent on the Front line Alec and his men were given a period of respite in bivouacs some three miles from the front. He had visited a small town, a jolly old place, and seen the church and houses in a state of destruction. He wrote to his father asking him to thank Maudie for the socks she had sent, As a matter of fact they are a trifle small but nevertheless v comfy.

Stanhope was reassured by the contents of a further letter which confirmed that Alec was still resting in camp, though he was aware that his son would soon be moving forward:

My dearest Dad

I found two lovely parcels waiting for me when we got down to rest last night. One with towels, socks, soap and books had been forwarded from Rouen, the other with more and excellent soap etc. arrived direct. It was nice of Fryn and Damit to send me socks and handkerchiefs – all most welcome. Then the books were two furniture books – sequels to the one I showed Stephen White – most interesting and showing the Queen Anne volume that our cabinet has quite typical cornice base and so on. I rather wish I could send you the books back but it isn't easy to send parcels at all. Although we are in such a very quiet part of the line it's a great treat to be in rest bivouacs again and to enjoy a regimental mess after a week of rations. I went down this morning and looked at a jolly old place with such a fine church now all battered to bits and the old house with windows smashed and boarded up – only a few French and British troops about. The countryside resembles a huge camp miles of bivouacs and depots and dumps– so different to the scenery 3 miles off – which is absolute desolation with patches of broken and torn trees and both sides British and German burrowing like moles throwing up each other all the most deadly engines of modern times.

By degrees we have got rid of the thick coating of mud which we brought back yesterday and after a vastly long night in luxurious tents with the great joy of having in bits again and sleeping in once more pink pyjamas. On the whole everyone is fairly well – our CO Colonel Fargus DSO is such a nice man and makes himself very pleasant to new subalterns.

9

Priceless to be Here – The Somme

On the morning of Sunday 2 September 1916, 2nd Lieutenant Forbes received a bundle of letters, some from Bedales girls, one from Fryn Jesse Tennyson and six letters from his father. He set about writing replies in pencil on thin paper:

1st DCLI BEF

My dearest Dad

Beyond an inspection of my platoon, a long conference with the C.O. which all officers attended and which if successful will make history – a communion service and a good deal of sleep. I haven't done much else today. – I have censored dozens and dozens of letters written by all the men, long sentimental screeds praying for the war to end. How ripping about Joe's Croix de la Guerre – very fine indeed of him to have won it. I will write to him as soon as ever can. Also to Nunkie. I enclose letter to Fryn I wish you would have delivered as I haven't the address of The Red House. Thank you so much for all these letters. I am so hugely grateful for them. I have spent a delightful afternoon reading them all thro and thro.

Love to all. Ever your loving Alec.

Those who waited back at home had always been ready to show their tangible support for the young man. Aware that the next day would see him taking part in one of biggest pushes of the war, Alec chose to use his letter to Fryn to send his thanks and a message of reassurance to his father:

1st DCLI 3.9.16 Sommewhere in France

Dear Fryn,

Thank you and Damit [17] (whose present and more proper name I never can remember, only you mustn't tell her so) hugely for the capital handkerchiefs and socks. It was ripping of you to send them out here and as I had just had such remarkable and luck with my hut as it was all buried by a shell smashing the parapet and smothering everything in Somme mud (the expression is of course American) that on our return to rest bivvys 2 days ago the socks and handkerchiefs came in for immediate use. I keep on impressing the professor that this is such a cushy part of the line. As a matter of fact if I become a casualty in the next few days it will be satisfactory to have gone under in one of the really biggest shows. I tried to tell him so today in the letter enclosing this but it is so difficult to anticipate events when writing to him. Perhaps you will give him the message.

Honestly though it is priceless to be here and as it's taken me so long to get here I appreciate it now. Thank you for speaking so of Mibbs – I do think she's jolly near us now and seems to help all the time.

Stanhope wrote on the envelope, *Addressed to Fryn Jesse enclosed in a letter to me written presumably Saturday the 2 Sept 1916, the eve of the battle in which he fell.* [18]

Later that day Alec led his men into battle. He carried with him some of his mother's jewellery. The *D.C.L.I.* regimental history records [19]:

3 Sept 1916. Night of the 2/3rd D.C.L.I. set out on their march to the front line trenches. They were in position by about 4 a.m. The main operations were due to begin at 12 noon and were to attack Falfemont Farm. Until it was attacked we were unable to advance towards Combles. With the exception of shell fire, which was always more or less heavy as the guns were seldom silent. The early morning of the 3rd was quiet and the weather fine. The Battalion is to go over in four waves.

All ranks were *full of confidence and in high spirits.*

At zero hour an intense artillery barrage was put down all along the German front and the troops advanced to the assault. So effective had been the fire of our guns that the first and second waves of Cornwalls, following quickly behind the barrage quickly captured the first objective. The third wave reached the line of the sunken road running south from Guillemont and took it the fourth then marched up the Bodmin trench.

The enemy met the advance with very heavy barrage but the Cornwalls pressed on steadily to their objective, quite undeterred. Even the storm of machine gun fire brought to bear on them failed to stop them, for the German machine gun teams were soon disposed of by rifle fire which showed the coolness and excellent marksmanship of the D.C.L.I. But it was during the advance to the first objective that most of the casualties to officers and men were sustained. Among them were four gallant young subalterns, all platoon commanders who fell at the head of their men, killed or mortally wounded they were 2 Lieutenant EGT Kitson, WAS Forbes JG Teage and WT Hutcheson.

Unaware of events in France, Stanhope continued to record the news he had received, though by now he must have been well aware of the danger his son faced:

September 3

Alec still in camp.

On 3 September Stanhope wrote to May:

Dearest May,

I was not greatly surprised to hear yesterday from my dear boy that he is in the trenches. It never seemed to me very probable that he would be kept for a long time at one of the bases. Perhaps because I felt it was too good to be true. But indeed I expect he would not have cared for this and would have grown impatient. His one wish all through has been to be with the best of his men doing his duty by their side and he has got his desire. He writes I need not say most cheerfully and it is impossible to feel other than most hopeful and confident after reading his letter. I daresay he has written to you but correspondence is not very easy under his present condition of life so I had better let you know his address is still 1ˢᵗ Batt D.C.L.I. 5ᵗʰ Division B.E.F. France.

Where he is I have no notion but it sounds as if it to be somewhere in the Somme front as he speaks of so much activity. But he assesses...

he is a couple of miles or so behind the front lines so that is consoling. And he adds that he has a really soft place. It doesn't sound like what I should consider so myself – but dear old chap he is full of joy at being in it.

But you are sure to hear soon. I do wish I could find out where he is – if by some means you can discover it you will be sure to let me know.

Ever yours affectionately Stanhope.

On September 5 Stanhope recorded:

Heard from Alec back in bivouac dated Sept. 2.

He is probably referring to a letter from Alec which had included a vivid account of life in the trenches and included a reflection on the beauty of the landscape,

Here is the constant crouching position while not walking about the trenches the rats are awful – but Tommy Atkins ever equal to the occasion fixes a bit of cheese

at the end of his bayonet — shoves same round the corner and waits. Presently Mr Rat arrives and starts to nibble the tempting morsel when the rude shock of a discharged rifle shakes his poor little body into the middle of next week. I am also by this time quite used to sleeping with my head tied up in a handkerchief to keep off all the flies! The landscape is wonderful — miles of tumbled earth — old Boche and British lines and heaps of rusty barbed wire — tall red weeds and red earth — some ruined villages and miles of torn tree trunks like desolate fingers. But the sky is the most impressive sight — this rainy weather has brought some very fine skies and big cumulous clouds…hosts of aeroplanes and observation balloons — with bursting shrapnel all round. We feel by looking up that ours is the mastery of the air and the constant strafe from our guns retaliated and some v poor and v inaccurate shots from Fritz shows all too clearly that its only a question of time and that as far as ascendancy is … it's our day at last. I do wish some of our pessimistic friends could come out here. It's ripping.

On the 6 Stanhope wrote to his brother:

Dear Bill

Many thanks for the wire. Maudie is most grateful to you. Very glad you also got news from Alec — Yesterday and today I have had two more letters. He had just got back to camp after a few days in the trenches and was enjoying good rest. Also I was delighted to hear some of our parcels had reached him. No doubt the books will fetch up in the mud — this morning there is a letter dated 30th which has taken a long time to reach me. He was then in the trenches and describes a German aviator being shot down. The fellow jumped out when about 2000 feet up with a parachute and came sailing down into his own lines. I am glad to hear the British troops cheered lustily. Alec describes his dug out which is a little tunnel about 5 ft wide 6ft long and 3ft 6 high and says is jolly snug. But the mud in the trenches is awful. He says the spirits of all are quite wonderful and they are certain of Victory. I do wish I could find out where he writes from but I feel quite sure it is somewhere near the Somme. As long as he is not in the front line I am thankful to know. I hope dearest Louise continues to get stronger each day. Still beastly weather here every day. Love to dear Louise. Ever yours Stan

May, who had become an important mentor and comforter for her cousin, wrote to Alec:

Bolderwood Sept 7 1916

Dearest Alec

Thanks so much for the card. Daddy sent me news also the badge. He is very good to me. I fancy he suspects I know secretly of your movements or whereabouts. But I assure him I don't at all. Here is the knife. I hope you will find it useful and find an occasion for all the implements. The button hook I am told is indispensible for pulling in boot laces when they are caked with mud. I should like to be a fly on your hat. Really know how you are fishing and how have you spend your time. I expect some of it is jolly horrid and patience trying. I wonder if you have actually seen or done any slaughtering yet? How I pity you for all the inevitable beastliness that must come your way. Saw those Somme films on Monday. They are really wonderful – not horrible at all – but very horrible.

Best love

Your loving Cousin, May Forbes

Stanhope's diary entries for 1916 come to an abrupt end on September 6. On September 7 he received a telegram:

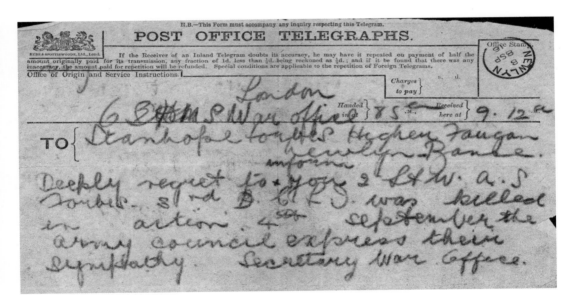

Transcript:
Deeply regret to inform you 2Lt W.A.S.Forbes was killed in action 4th September
(the inaccurate date is an error by the War Office)
the Army Council expresses their sympathy. Secretary War office.

On 8 Sept, Colonel Fargus, Alec's commanding officer, wrote:

Dear Mr Forbes

I deeply regret to have to inform you that your son was killed in action on September 3. He was killed at the head of his platoon while leading them to the assault. He had not been with me very long, but I had already formed a most favourable opinion of him and regarded him as one of my most promising officers. He took his platoon over in a most gallant way. He is buried close to where he fell not far from and a little to the south of Guillemont. It may help you in your loss – as your boy contributed to It – to know that the regiment did magnificently that day and captured all their objectives. Please accept on behalf of myself and the regiment our deepest sympathy with you and your family.

Yours sincerely

Harold Fargus

Lt. Col. 3rd Bn. Duke of Cornwall's Light Infantry.

The Keeper of the Privy Purse sent a letter of consolation from the King and Queen:

The King and Queen deeply regret the loss you...have and the...have sustained by the death of your son in the service of his country. Their majesties truly sympathise with you in your sorrow.

Fryn Jesse described Stanhope's reaction on hearing the news [20]: op.cit.

May was making blackberry jam, and I shall always link the smell of blackberry jelly in warm sunshine with the news I was given...I borrowed a trap from nearby farmer, and drove to Faugan. Maudie was in tears, took me up to the bedroom where Stan was lying in the big double bed. He was distraught, grieving for Mibbs all over again as well as Alec. What he wanted me to do was to take all the flowers that Maudie and I could pick to Sancreed churchyard and put great bunches on Mibb's grave in memory of Alec.'

She wrote to her father on 14 September,

Darlingest – I am rather dead after five awful days with poor Stan. I have never seen such agony of grief. It has been enough to tear one's heart out to be with him. What he would have done without Maudie I don't know. He asked me to write an appreciation of dear Alec for the local papers; the most difficult thing I have ever done.

Alec's grave marked with a wooden cross which had been placed by the Royal Engineers. It is now in Sancreed Church next to Alec's memorial
Private collection

Alec's grandmother, Bonne Mama, wrote [21], *His life was indeed full of thought for his dear father and it was reciprocated. I never knew such love or devotion.*

Maudie commented:

> *Stan is so brave and takes his overwhelming sorrow so beautifully, but at times it is almost more than his dear heart can bear. It breaks my heart to see his anguish. I loved that dear boy so dearly. He was always so sweet to me and I was always so grateful to him for it.*

Stanhope's brother went immediately down to Newlyn and described his visit in a letter to May:

> *Sept 11 1916*
>
> *189 Maida Vale*
>
> *My dearest May*
>
> *I have just returned from Newlyn and am so glad my wife was able to spare me for 48 hours to see poor and stricken Stan. He was just a crushed bundle of humanity sitting in his bedroom in his dressing gown when I arrived. He is now up and about*

and yesterday we spent hours together in the garden that Alec loved so well.

When he has got over his agony he will hold his head high when he talks of his noble boy. Alec got a bundle of letters from his Dad on Sunday the 3rd Sept. and was so rejoiced to be able to read them. On the afternoon he received with his comrades the communion and an inspiring address from his Colonel for the great event that was to follow on the morrow. He was so proud and happy to be in it but you must read his last letters to realise his great happiness and his preparation for the great sacrifice. I am so glad to think that dear Stan had painted a beautiful portrait of him some few months ago. It is in the studio with a laurel wreath of flowers that he loved all around it. You must come and see us. Louise is bearing up bravely but is very weak and has not closed an eye since I left. I am now going up to her and feel sure she will sleep but felt I must send you a line to tell of my dear brother. He will write you himself. I got your letter at Newlyn. Maudie, his wife, has been splendid and is so gentle and tender with dear Stan that she is a great help to him. Mother is wonderful and only breaks down when she sees Stan's distress. She was up at 7.30 this morning and accompanied me to the station. She also got your letter and was so pleased that I had written her.

God bless you. Come soon.

Your affectionate cousin

William Forbes

It is not difficult to imagine the confusion on the battlefield. Thousands of men fell and were left unburied. The enemy was able to target any grave digging parties. Many men were never identified and their families were left to grieve without even the consolation of knowing where the mortal remains of their loved ones rested.

Stanhope experienced initial frustration in attempting to discover the location of Alec's grave. The War Office wrote *I am sorry to hear how uncertain you are about where your dear boy's grave is.* He was however, fortunate to receive a letter from a Roman Catholic priest, Lt O'Connor, on 16 October [22]:

In the short time he was with us we had all learnt to respect him as a thoroughly sweet, conscientious, brave man. It was impossible to carry the dead from the field during extensive operation. When burial becomes impossible a great many cannot be identified.

O'Connor describes how he found Alec's body on the 4 September and buried him where he lay, *The dead lie unburied for weeks. He lies where he fell* [23].

The Germans soon overran the place where Alec lay and it was a week before the priest was able to search again for the burial site. The Royal Engineers placed a wooden cross over the grave. Consoled by the news that Alec's body and grave had been identified, Stanhope wrote:

> Now at least I know how glorious was his end and I know where my darling rests. We know what he felt and thought that last Sunday his pride in being in one of the big things of this war and can realise his joy when that supreme moment in his life came and he did his duty like the brave English gentleman he was.

Some of Alec's possessions were recovered and listed on 25 September as :*a pocket book(diary), a cheque book, 1 officer's advance book, 1 Book of Common Prayer, 1 Idenitity disk, 1 small key, 15 centimes and private letters* [24] *and photos.*

Stanhope was, however, dismayed to hear the items of jewellery and other valuables had been taken. A letter from O'Connor written on Jan 15 1917 brought an answer to his questioning:

> I have to tell you frankly what I hope you in particular and the people at home would never know. Nearly every dead man's body is robbed. Nearly every dead officer had been robbed. Your son's pockets had been emptied and even his revolver had been taken. I am deeply sorry that you have not been spared this further pain. There are men who are so brutal and callous as to loot their own dead comrades.

A soldier was found in possession of two letters and it was thought the same man might have been responsible for the looting. O'Connor thought it unlikely.

Stanhope also heard from Charlie Lambert, Alec's friend who had joined them for an outing while Alec was training on the Isle of Wight. He had been sent to the school of oriental studies to learn Arabic. He wrote of E.G. Templeton Kitson, who had died with Alec on the 3rd, *Kitson was a great friend of Alec's at Freshwater. They both belonged to the 3rd Battalion DCLI and went to the 1st.*

Correspondence from Stanhope's Cousin Frank refers to attempts to mark Alec's grave and acquire a photograph of it:

> My Dear Stan, I will get the inscription put on the cross erected. I am afraid a photo is at present unobtainable as no British Officer is allowed to have a camera.

The letter goes on to give a vivid description of the scene at the Front:

> The cold out here is really awful but there is a bright side. The frost has made the mud and slime like iron so we can walk now instead of wading.

It is a wonderful scene from artists' point of view, looking out over No Man's Land, but I have looked at it for over two years and mostly in the same place and am very tired of it. June 1918 will see the end of it. Earlier than that is impossible.

Stanhope was not the only one who was left uncertain and unconsoled by the War Office. He corresponded with other grieving parents and they supported each other. John Skillcorn wrote:

We stayed with the French people until Thursday and we went every day and watered the flowers on your boy's grave and our own. We think your boy's grave may be in the photo is it is so near the entrance to the cemetery at Guillemont. Some day please God if we keep our health we will be able to visit Guillemont again. It is all we have to live and work for.

John Skillcorn, County Durham. Father of John Skillcorn 12949 L/Cpl Signaller.

In March 1918 the family of a soldier who had died alongside Alec forwarded correspondence from Pioneer H Moyle [25] which gave a detailed account of events:

Mar. 6 1918

Pioneer H. Moyle 31754

1st D.C.L.I.

Transport I.E.F.

Italy

Dear Mr and Mrs Prowse,

Just a line or two about your son Arthur. We trained together and went into action together and he was very lucky he was a nice chap indeed we always got on alright. I used to like him and I know he liked me ever so much. Well when we went over the tip at Guillemont we was together and one of our officers (Alec) got wounded and he helped one or two more fellows to carry him to the dressing station and after carrying him a little way they stopped to have a rest and a great shell came over and killed poor Arthur and three more and I helped to bury him and I never saw a mark more than a scratch on his arm he had a nice little grave and his name on it so that I can tell you will find that correct.

The account was not wholly consistent with the information Stanhope had received from Lt O'Connor, who had apparently buried Alec early in the morning after the battle. Alec's grave was located near a sunken road and not in it, as Moyle had suggested in earlier correspondence [26].

In May 1919 Stanhope was at last able to visit the site. He wrote to Mr Prowse:

22 May 1919

Higher Faugan

Newlyn

Dear Mr Prowse

I am able to give you the following information but must ask you to regard it as strictly confidential. I was able a little more than a fortnight ago to get over to France, my brother has important official work which sometimes takes him across and on one of his visits he was able to take me with him. We stayed a night at Amiens and the next day we got a car and motored to the Somme battlefield where by great fortune I was able to find my dear son's grave, I found it impossible to locate any other graves but possibly the following particulars which I am able to give you may be of some little comfort to you as I gather your son is buried close to where my son lies. I must have been very near to him and doubtless one of those many crosses I saw around me must mark his resting place. You will easily understand that I found it a most terrible ordeal and indeed I scarcely was able to endure it but I am very thankful that I was able to go. But even if I had found it less trying I don't think I could, without precise information, have found any particular grave. They are simply endless and as far as the eye can see on all sides in that dreadful scene of desolation, the little white crosses are to be seen, sometimes scattered, at other places in large groups, just around Guillemont they are particularly thick and I have great hopes that owing to this they may possibly be allowed to remain undisturbed. I do not know your feelings, but my own are very strongly for leaving them where they lie on the glorious battlefield.

The graves, I may tell you, are mostly, indeed almost all in quite good condition and although the Germans retook that part and were afterwards driven out they have evidently respected our soldiers graves. There are indeed a good many of their own men lying there amongst our boys. As for the place itself it is quite indescribable – The desolation and havoc is beyond anything words can convey. We drove through Albert, one of the last towns to be destroyed, and there is not one single house standing in it and after leaving it, as we got nearer to Guillemont the devastation became worse and worse, But it is all quiet now, the men lie at rest undisturbed, not a soul to be seen for miles around, only the birds singing above the ground where they lie. The field has of course been tidied though to me it looked almost as if the battle had been fought a few weeks since.

I think this is one reason why they will still allow no one to visit it for there are plenty of unexploded bombs and shells lying about. This is also why I ask you to regard my letter as confidential, I had really no right to be there but I don't suppose anyone would blame me for having managed to get over. When the time comes, as it will I believe very soon, that permission will be given, I shall be most happy to send you more particulars which may help you in your search. I can anyhow tell you how to find the sunken road for my son lies close to it, I was fortunate in hearing from the Chaplain who buried him very soon after the battle and it's entirely owing to that I have been able to find the grave.

The sunken road runs from the corner of what was once Guillemont in a south westerly direction. Our boys lie a few hundred yards nearly due south of what is known as Trones Wood this can still be located by the trunks of the trees. Of Guillemont itself, beyond the name written on a notice board, not a vestige remains. Amiens is the nearest place where you can stay but it is between 30 and 40 miles and one can only get to the battlefield by motor car.

I am deeply grieved I can give you no further information but rest assured that your boy's grave is now undisturbed and being looked after for one can see that they are all being attended to. You can also feel pretty confident that it has not been injured for scarcely any show any sign of serious damage.

Yours very sincerely

Stanhope A Forbes

Stanhope received a further letter from Lt O'Connor, following his visit to Guillemont:

15 July 1919,

The sight of the battlefield made a deep impression on you as I know it must on a man of your sensitive nature. Only a vision could inspire such an utter renunciation in a sensitive mind and frame like Alec's. He achieved the highest possible act of man.

10

Memories and Memorials

The cross erected by the Royal Engineers on Alec's grave was brought back to England and stands today in the church at Sancreed. Stanhope supervised the creation of a remarkable memorial to Alec. Unveiled in the little church on March 17 1920, it was designed by Mr Edward Warren FSA and included a cast bronze image of Alec based on the painting Stanhope had worked on during Alec's Christmas leave in 1915. Maudie and Stanhope added an inscription. The words were taken from a letter written by Denis Garstin after meeting with Alec in France [(27)]:

> He saw beyond the filth of battle and thought death a fair price to pay to belong to the company of these fellows.

The memorial was framed by marble columns from Derbyshire and included maple leaves as a reference to Elizabeth's Canadian heritage. Stanhope later admitted that working on the memorial had eased the grieving process. On the Sunday following the unveiling he was arrived late arriving for the morning service and as he entered the church he heard the Rev Stona reading the first lesson. The first words he heard were, *this is my memorial unto all generations* (Exodus 3 v 15)

Fryn Tennyson Jesse reluctantly agreed to Stanhope's request that she write an obituary for the *Cornishman*. It was published on September 14:

> On September 4 there fell in action William Alexander Stanhope Forbes (Alec) only child of Stanhope Forbes R.A. The brief statement of such a death is, as expressed in the official telegram – 'fell in action' – is in itself a paean and a requiem. It has come to be recognised as the finest and the saddest phrase in the world. There were, in connection with Alec Forbes circumstances which went to make it, if possible, even finer than usual. If anyone can be said to have an excuse for not serving, this boy, who was only twenty-three when he fell, had every excuse. He was so delicate that when he tried to enlist at the outbreak of war he could not pass the medical test and had to undergo an operation and treatment to enable him to do so eventually. He was not merely an only child but the last male representative of his line in this generation; and after doing very well at Bedales College, where he was educated, he went on to take, in 1914, the highest honour open to him at this stage in his profession – he won

the Travelling scholarship of the Architectural Association. When he recovered from the effects of his operation he was given a lieutenants commission in the Military Forwarding Establishment and served in it in France. But he considered he was not doing his duty while serving in one of the 'safe jobs' and at his own request was transferred into the third battalion of the D.C.L.I. When he was sent to France he was drafted in to the First Battalion, a circumstance which gave him almost as much pleasure as being at last at the Front. He was not three weeks there before he was killed.

'De Mortuis nil nisi bonum' is so much an accepted axiom that it tends to draw, if not discredit, at least the tolerance of a kindly disbelief, but it was only necessary to know slightly Alec Forbes to realise that in praise of him the old adage would hold no part. It is easy to point to this or that person and say of him that he has courage or honesty or purity, but with Alec Forbes it was not so much that he had these excellencies as that he possessed the quality of goodness. There are, luckily for world, many very good people who live long and helpful lives, overcoming temptations, but some there are who seem set apart, past whom the breath of evil goes like an idle wind, and of them we say, in the old common parlance which never knocked at the heart with sharper foreboding than when Alec Forbes went to the Front, that they were too good for this world – the gods love them and they die young.

With all his brilliance and sense of humour, Alec Forbes had the highest simplicity that never sees but the one way and, seeing it, takes it. In a book which had a great vogue years before he was born, such a character is spoken of as being a 'courtier in the household of god'. Alec Forbes had no doubts about his duty, he went into no high-flown ecstasies of patriotism, nor was he ever, with all his gentleness, tainted by the selfishness of the pacifist. He was one of the courtiers of the household of God, and with straight unfaltering feet he had passed the threshold of its inner temple.

And to him who is left behind and to whom has come his son's last message of considerate thoughtfulness, it is possible, in cardinal Mercier's phrase of immortal pride to offer not only condolence, but congratulations. F. Tennyson Jesse [28]

On September 10, 1916, May Forbes received a letter from her friend Rachael:

My darling

Your letter came to me in the silence we keep after our peaceful and wonderful mass out in the tent.

Do you remember that we were together when you had his telegram saying he was going? And do you remember our drive home from Milford and the wonderful sky? And you talked of him then and said you felt sure he was not coming home. Now he has gone straight home – with his pure clean soul unstained and unspoilt by all *the horror and misery of war. You must be so thankful he was out there such a short time. I think God must have loved him too much to let him be out there long. He must have wanted him near himself. To help those poor souls who fall in battle. And who have not the same purity as Alex when they go over the other side. It is just lovely to think of those officers, meeting their men and going on with their training under that other captain. But my May you will miss him so much: your boy who was so much to you. It must be rather wonderful though – to think of all those last years and all the time together and all you taught him of the things that matter more than death. And I expect his mother is just loving you for it. Now that she is with her son again.*

The family were keen to acknowledge the part played by the 'girl' who had first captured the heart of young Alec. Stanhope wrote to May:

I want to tell you how much I shall feel the deepest gratitude for the love you gave him. When his mother died he came through that awful trial I know the gap in his life would be a dreadful one. But you helped so much to fill it and, May dear, I am sure you are proud of the work you did for the great influence you always had upon him helped to form that noble sweet nature. I remember to treasure greatly the recollection of how you have talked of him, how you loved and understood him and I bless you for it dear. [29]

Maudie wrote movingly:

Higher Faugan

Newlyn

Wednesday

Dearest May (from Maudie)

I had meant to write today to you so that I know you will be anxious for news of my darling Stan and then your letter came. Thank you so much for it you have been a great deal in our thoughts as we know what a sorrow this is to you too, it must be a great comfort to you to feel how devoted the sweet boy was to you and how much you helped him on his way. God help us dear May. I know you will pray for us. I loved the dear boy so dearly, it was such a joy to me to have the right to care and love him for a little while.

With the exception of Mibbs and his grandmother, there were two women who had played a significant part in helping to form Alec's views and character: Mabel and May. Shortly after hearing of Alec's death Mabel wrote to May:

My faith in God seemed shattered May – will He forgive me? – and I was bitter bitter! Me who thought I understood and professed to teach my little Alec the love of God – your letter came in time I think dear May. I must be far from feeling a Christian at heart and it is sweet of you to think as you do of my influence on my darling Alec. I on the other side have always felt that you had a great deal to do with the forming of Alec's character and personality – you came into his life as he was leaving childhood behind – you helped him to bear the great sorrow of his life May – and your friendship has to a great extent made our dear boy what he was. So I will try like you to not be selfish and to think of him as being reunited to his dear mother in a better world.

The gross value of Alec's estate on his death was £9586. This was twice the value of his mother's estate on her death and the equivalent of perhaps half a million pounds today. He bequeathed £200 to Mabel Gibbs, £200 to Nurse Kelly *in recognition of her attention to my late mother* and £100 to the Architectural Association for the educational purposes of the Association, a legacy of £100 to the funds of the Artists General Benevolent Association. Three of the pictures belonging to him and painted by his late mother were bequeathed to his uncle and aunt, Sir William and Lady Forbes. Cousin May was to receive any three of the pictures belonging to him and painted by his mother. The remainder of his estate was bequeathed to his father.

Alec also left £100 to the trustees of Bedales School with any of his books the librarian of the school chose to select. The *Bedales Chronicle* noted:

The library has been very much increased this term, owing to the books left us by Forbes – by far the best gift it has ever had. We could not be more fortunate in the collection, as it contains the most beautiful books on architecture and art in general.

By the wish of all it has been decided that they should form one collection, so that in the new library to come a whole group of shelves will be allotted to them alone.

No gift could have been more universal, nor one that reminds us so much of the giver.

And:

Alec Forbes, Mr Badley learns from his father, has left £50 to the school, and 'such of his books as you care to select' We take this opportunity of expressing on behalf of the whole school the pride we feel in such a bequest. We do not yet know what form of memorial the money gift may take but it will surely be some permanent enrichment of the school life which Bedalians past, present and to come, may connect with his name and these days of sacrifice. Perhaps a bay in that new school library, which just before August 1914 it seemed might become something more tangible than a castle in the air.

Of the sacrifice made by Alec and many other Bedalians, J. H. Badley wrote:

For us they have added a new splendour to life, and have helped to shape that finer world for which it is worthwhile to make even this sacrifice; and for themselves surely it is no end, but a beginning, and we can bid them –

Speed, fight on, fare ever

There as here!'

The *Architectural Association* published an obituary in their in house magazine, in which the contributor unerringly captured the sense of Alec's 'boyishness' and kindness:

W. A. Stanhope Forbes

An Appreciation

The news of the death of W.A.S. Forbes, on active service, will come as a severe shock to all those whose privilege it was top know him at the A.A., and indeed in many instances, as in that of a writer, as a personal loss and grief. In Forbes the A.A. loses one of its most promising students and a charming personality – charming in the respect that no one who came in touch with him could fail to be impressed by the totally unaffected and inspiriting enthusiasm and joie de vivre which he possessed and which characterised his work and everything he did. On looking at his work, replete with imagination, this trait showed itself most clearly and made one long for closer acquaintance with the author.

To me, as well as many others of his year, his sad loss will be keenly regretted and his place at the A.A. will never be filled simply because he possessed a nature so full of unassuming kindness and ' boyishness' of a character which is rarely met with. A brilliant student, possessing an inexhaustible stock of ideas, he will be long remembered at the A.A. not only for his enthusiasm but for several exceptional designs. Capable both as a draughtsman and colourist, it was principally as a colourist that he excelled, and there was a tendency to sacrifice possible general excellence of his work to the exercise of this gift, but as time went on an even balance of all essentials took place and with such results as to make both fellow students and those who taught him rebel at the mere thought of such possibilities cut short.

But we must bow our heads to the inevitable, though with feelings of regretful anger and grief at a shining light, which he would undoubtedly have been to his profession had he been spared, being extinguished.

To a very few he was known as 'Forbes', to the majority as 'Willie', as he was affectionately named. To all his loss is very keenly felt, but to myself and many other friends who knew him perhaps still better his loss is irreparable.

Niel Koch

Recognising that Alec had been denied the opportunity to use the scholarship prize to enjoy travelling through Europe, the Architectural Association commissioned a stained-glass window to present to his grieving father The window was designed and made by Dudley Forsyth.

On receiving the window Stanhope wrote:

Yesterday afternoon Mr Mackenzie called bringing with him the very beautiful little stained glass window which the Architectural Association have so very kindly presented to. Words fail me to express how very deeply grateful I am for this charming gift.

Eight years after Alec's death Stanhope received one of many letters written by those who remembered Alec:

The Elms

Bedhampton

Hants

6.3.24

Dear Sir,

I was dining with Mr Wyllie at Tower House a few days ago and we were talking of your boy who was in my school of Instruction at Portsmouth before going out to France and Mrs Wyllie told me how much you had felt his loss and that it would comfort you to know what a high opinion I formed of him during the 5 weeks he was under me.

He was one of the best young officers I had. In the 13 months I must have had between 500 and 1000. He often came to this house on a Sat afternoon and was a favourite with Lady Constance and my two girls.

I had a high opinion of his ability as well as his character. I used to take a few at a time over a farm where the undulating ground was difficult to contour and show them how to interpolate contours on an enlargement of the 1 inch map and so show ground which the 100ft contours did not show and he was the only one that I can remember in all the 13 months who surveyed a piece of ground afterwards by himself and did very well. I can feel for you in your loss as since then I have lost both my daughters who were full of life.

Your boy died for his country in the Great War and only those who realise what a near thing it was and what we should have suffered as a nation had the Germans won must ever remember with gratitude at what cost of young life it was done. My comfort in sorrow has been that verse in Corinthians, Our light affliction, which is for a moment, worketh for us, a far more exceeding and eternal weight of glory, while we look not at the things which are seen, but at the things which are not seen. *I have been a great admirer of your talent ever since I saw your picture of the blacksmiths shop. I think you had a cousin of mine as a pupil at Newlyn, Miss Fawkes.*

Believe me

Yours very sincerely

LG Fawkes Col. Late R.A.

On 10 November 1925 Stanhope received a letter from Lt O'Connor:

I am so glad you have the cross the engineers put on Alec's grave. It is another close link with him. I Think you have found it the right setting at Sancreed. There, too, it will be a lasting memorial. I remember being struck by its fineness. It was one of the best temporary crosses I saw. I feel grateful that my little improvised and very perishable cross led to it.

The cross still stands inside the old church.

Sometime after his son's death Stanhope wrote:

This is always a sad season for me though indeed I miss him all the time – But I have his happy life to look back upon to remember that he has been spared all the disenchantments, all the disappointments which a nature like his must have had to endure.

Do you know Robert Louis Stevenson's lovely little poem beginning –

Yet O stuck in heart remember, O remember

How of human days he lived the better part.

April came to bloom and never dim December

Breathed its killing chills upon the head or heart.

After the war Stanhope set up an appeal fund for the erection of a Newlyn War Memorial, *there being not much support from the people of Newlyn.* Interestingly Stanhope asked a student at the Architectural Association, Edward Warren, to design the memorial. Edward's teacher, Leonard Merrifield, fashioned the bronze plaque.

Stanhope's diaries record that every year on the anniversary of Alec's death, he went to Sancreed with Maudie. Shortly after the war he was able to reflect on his treasured memories, *What a legacy he left me in that fine and spotless life which I rejoice to see have seen him live* [(30)]

Stanhope lived on to a good age. His diaries continued. Perhaps the most poignant entry appears on September 3 1939:

Sunday, September 3 1939. War declared 11.15 a.m. As we start for Sancreed this day the anniversary of my son's death I hear from Spurgs that war is to be declared at 11.15 on our return we learn that it has been done and England and Germany are again at war...an unforgettable morning in our lives.' [(31)]

Alec's grave in the cemetery at Guillemont
Private Collection

Endnotes

1 For a more detailed description of Bedales and its founder see *The Neo-Pagans. Friendship and Love in the Rupert Brooke Circle*. Paul Delaney. Macmillan 1987

2 *Oil Paint and Grease Paint* The Autobiography of Laura Knight. Nicholson and Watson 1936

3 Quoted in *A Portrait of Fryn. A Biography of F. Tennyson Jesse*. Joanna Colenbrander. Andre Deutsch. 1984

4 Alec recorded this memory on March 2nd 1916

5 The '*dumps*' is a term used by Stanhope to describe periods of depression he often experienced

6 The Architectural Association. Obituary 1916. Quoted in full in Chapter 11

7 The title of Stanhope's painting exhibited at the R.A. in 1915

8 The Altar frontal is still used on occasions in Sancreed Church

9 Tate Britain TGA 9015/4/6-3

10 Tate Archive 9015.2.1.507

11 Alec was the model for the boy looking into a dark wood in his mother's charcoal drawing for *King Arthur's Wood – On the other side of the stile was a whole new world*. In 1904 Mrs Lionel Birch commented on the drawing in her biography of Stanhope and Elizabeth: *Something about it makes me afraid*.

12 I.G.C. The Inspector General of Communications

13 Lt Glyn. He had been an engineer on the London Brighton and South Coast Railway

14 Harry Jacob. A former student at the Architectural Association. He served in the 15th Hants.

15 Tate Britain TGA 9015/3/19/34

16 The Tate Archives 9015.4.6/6

17 Damit was Sybil Sampson. One of the art students staying at Myrtle Cottage, Newlyn, had, as Fryn records, 'a trick of talking in double inversion between ourselves, and we became so adept at it that we rarely fell into normal speech'. Mrs Forbes became Forces Mibbs.

18 The Tate Archives 9015.4.6.7

19 Unit War diaries held at The National Archive (WO 95/1577/2) and recorded in Everard Wyrall, *The Duke of Cornwall's Light Infantry 1914-1919*, Methuen 1932

20 Quoted in *A Portrait of Fryn. A Biography of F. Tennyson Jesse*. Joanna Colenbrander. Andre Deutsch. 1984

21 Letter from Stanhope's mother to Miss Focher 17th September 1916

22 Tate Britain TGA 9015/3/12

23 Tate Britain TGA 9015/3/12

24 Two bloodstained letters were found on his body

25 Pioneer Harry Moyle 31754, 1st D.C.L.I. Transport I.E.F. wrote from Italy.

26 Arthur Prowse is buried at Thiepval Memorial Cemetery a few kilometres from Guillemont.

27 Letter from Denys Garstin describing the meeting at Hazebruck, written from Petrograd in Sept 1917.

28 Fryn Tennyson Jesse was a notable poet and writer. She was a close friend of Alec, having known him for many years. In a letter dated 16 August 1916 Alec wrote, *Thanks for Fryniwyd's ripping little poem.*

29 May never married. She was brought up in a 'grace and favour' apartment in Hampton Court. She became a missionary, lived in Folkestone and died in 1964

30 Letter from Stanhope to Cousin May, 21st Dec 1921

31 The Tate Archive 9019.1.1

Sources

The National Archives, Kew, London. Unit War Diaries, Long Service papers (W.O 95, W.O. 372, W.O. 339)

Tate Britain Archive (TGA 9015)

Cornwall's Regimental Museum, Bodmin

Penlee House Gallery and Museum / Forbes family archive

The Imperial War Museum

The Architectural Association, London

Sancreed Church, Cornwall

The Bedales Schools, Hampshire

Bibliography

Stanhope and Elizabeth Forbes, Mrs Lionel Birch (Cassell and Co 1906), reprinted Truran 2005

Oil Paint and Grease Paint, Dame Laura Knight, Nicholson and Watson, London 1936

A Portrait of Fryn, Joanna Colenbrander, Andre Deutsch 1984

The Duke of Cornwall's Light Infantry 1914-1918, Everard Wyrall, Methuen 1932

The Neo Pagans, Paul Delany, Macmillan 1987

Life, Death and Growing Up on the Western Front, Anthony Fletcher, Yale 2013

Acknowledgements

I would like to thank the following for their advice, practical support and encouragement:

The Forbes Family:

Fi Carpenter (Stanhope's great-niece) who shared her knowledge of the family and allowed me access to her extensive written and photographic archive.

Harriet Graham, Adam Woolfitt and Paul Bangay (members of the Forbes family) for advising on family history and sharing written and photographic archive material.

Penlee House Gallery and Museum:

Katie Herbert (Curator / Deputy Director) who gave encouragement, sound advice and displayed exceptional professionalism and patience in assisting with handling resources.

Richard Nesham (Technical Officer) for using his expertise to scan and enhance many fading images.

Louise Connell (Director) for allowing me access to Penlee's archive facilities.

Jenny Fitton (volunteer), who was always willing to assist with interpretation of (sometimes opaque!) written material.

Ron Clegg (volunteer), who did so much initial work on the Forbes archive.

The Architectural Association, London:

Edward Bottoms (Archivist, History and Theory Studies tutor), for allowing me to visit the A.A. archive and for assisting with documents and photographic images.

Cornwall's Regimental Museum, Bodmin (a wonderful museum!):

Mary Godwin (Director)

Major Hugo White D.C.L.I.

Bedales School, Hampshire:

Jane Kirby, Librarian and Archivist

Military and Local Historians:

Major Bob Harrison

Alan and Diana Shears (Art Historians) for sharing their extensive archive

Pam Lomax, Ron Hogg, David Tredinnick, Diane Tredinnick, Bill Royston,

Kelvin Hearn and Linda Holmes for their practical support and encouragement.

Truran:

Heather and Ivan Corbett, for their willingness and professional approach to the publication of Alec's story and their patience in listening to my endless stream of Alec anecdotes.

Index of People and Places